Contents

Introduction

One of the quickest, easiest, and most versatile methods of cooking is to cook in a wok. It takes only a few minutes to assemble the ingredients— a selection of vegetables, to which may be added meat, fish, shellfish, bean curd, nuts, rice, or noodles. The possibilities are endless for  ringing the changes with different oils, seasonings, and sauces, and the result is a colorful, delicious, healthy meal.

Although the wok can be used for steaming and deep-frying, its main use is for stir-frying. As it cooks, the food is tossed and turned with long bamboo chopsticks, a wok scoop, or spatula.

Some foods need a slightly longer cooking time than others and, for this reason, cooking is often done in stages. This also allows the individual ingredients to retain their distinct flavors. As they cook, the foods are removed from the wok, but they are always combined once everything is cooked, and served as a whole dish.

There is plenty of scope for creativity when choosing ingredients, even for the simplest stir-fry. A combination of onions, carrots, bell peppers (green, red, yellow, and orange), broccoli, and snow peas will provide the basis for a colorful dish. Add bean sprouts at the end of cooking and toss quickly for texture, or some canned water chestnuts, which add a delicious crunch. A few cashews or almonds, some bean curd or boneless chicken, or a handful of shrimp provide protein, while adding some precooked rice or noodles makes a gutsy stir-fry. A sauce—perhaps oyster or yellow bean—will finish off the dish. Ginger, garlic, and chiles are wonderful for flavoring stir-fries.

Chiles come in a wide variety, ranging in heat from very mild to fiery hot. The Thai's favor the small red or green "bird-eye" chiles, which are very fiery, and their curries are flavored with ferociously hot chili pastes. Crushed dried chilies are also useful for seasoning. Some of the "kick" can be taken out of a hot chile by removing the seeds and mambrane. Cut fresh chiles in half, and scrape out the seeds with the point of a knife. Cut off the end of dried chilies and shake out the seeds. Always wash your hands after handling chilies!

Basic Recipes

Fresh Chicken Bouillon

MAKES 7½ CUPS

2 lb 4 oz/1 kg chicken, skinned

2 celery stalks

1 onion

2 carrots

1 garlic clove

few fresh parsley sprigs

9 cups water

salt and pepper

1 Put all the ingredients into a large pan.

2 Bring to a boil. Skim away any surface scum with a large flat spoon. Reduce the heat to a gentle simmer, partially cover, and cook for 2 hours. Let cool.

3 Line a strainer with clean cheesecloth and place over a large pitcher or bowl. Pour the liquid through the strainer. The cooked chicken can be used in another recipe. Discard the other solids. Cover the stock and chill.

4 Skim away any fat that forms before using. Store in the refrigerator for 3–4 days, until required, or freeze in small batches.

Fresh Fish Bouillon

MAKES 7½ CUPS

1 head of a cod or salmon, etc, plus the trimmings, skin, and bones or just the trimmings, skin, and bones

1–2 onions, sliced

1 carrot, sliced

1–2 celery stalks, sliced

good squeeze of lemon juice

1 bouquet garni envelope or 2 fresh or dried bay leaves

1 Wash the fish head and trimmings and place in a large pan. Add sufficient water to cover and bring to a boil.

2 Skim away any surface scum with a large flat spoon, then add the remaining ingredients. Cover and let simmer for about 30 minutes.

3 Strain and cool. Store in the refrigerator and use within 2 days.

Cornstarch Paste

Cornstarch paste is made by mixing 1 part cornstarch with about 1½ parts of cold water. Stir until smooth. The paste is used to thicken sauces.

Fresh Vegetable Bouillon

This can be kept chilled for up to three days or frozen for up to three months. Salt is not added when cooking the bouillon: it is better to season it according to the dish in which it is to be used.

MAKES 6¼ CUPS
9 oz/250 g shallots
1 large carrot, diced
1 celery stalk, chopped
½ fennel bulb
1 garlic clove
1 bay leaf
few fresh parsley and tarragon sprigs
8¾ cups water
pepper

1 Put all the ingredients in a large pan and bring to a boil.

2 Skim away any surface scum with a large flat spoon. Reduce the heat to a gentle simmer, partially cover, and cook for 45 minutes. Let cool.

3 Line a strainer with clean cheesecloth and put over a large pitcher or bowl. Pour the liquid through the strainer. Discard the herbs and vegetables.

4 Cover and store in the refrigerator for up to 3 days or freeze in small batches.

Fresh Coconut Milk

To make it from fresh grated coconut, place about 3 cups grated coconut in a bowl, pour over about 2½ cups boiling water to just cover, and let stand for 1 hour. Strain through cheesecloth, squeezing hard to extract as much "thick" milk as possible. If you require coconut cream, let stand, then skim the "cream" from the surface for use. Dry unsweetened coconut can also be used in the same quantities.

Soups & Appetizers

Soup is indispensable at Asian tables, especially in China, Japan, Korea, and South-East Asia. It is generally eaten part way through a main meal to clear the palate for further dishes. There are many different types of delicious soups, both thick and thin and, of course, the clear soups, which are often served with wontons or dumplings.

Appetizers or snacks are drier foods in general; the spring roll is a well-known Chinese snack and these come in many variations and shapes across the Far East. Other delights are wrapped in pastry, bread, and rice paper or are skewered for ease of eating; vegetables, fish, and meat are also deep-fried for a crispy coating. These dishes are served as starters in Westernized restaurants to animate the taste buds for the main course.

spicy thai soup with shrimp

serves four

2 tbsp tamarind paste

4 fresh red chiles, seeded and very
finely chopped

2 garlic cloves, minced

2 tsp finely chopped Thai ginger

4 tbsp Thai fish sauce

2 tbsp palm sugar or
superfine sugar

5 cups fish bouillon

8 kaffir lime leaves

1 large carrot, very thinly sliced

2 cups diced sweet potatoes

3½ oz/100 g halved baby corn cobs

3 tbsp coarsely chopped
fresh cilantro

3½ oz/100 g cherry
tomatoes, halved

8 oz/225 g fan-tail shrimp

1 Place the tamarind paste, red chiles, garlic, ginger, fish sauce, sugar, and fish bouillon in a preheated wok or large heavy skillet. Tear the lime leaves and add to the wok. Bring to a boil, stirring constantly to blend the flavors.

2 Reduce the heat and add the carrots, sweet potatoes, and baby corn cobs to the mixture in the wok.

3 Simmer the soup, uncovered, for about 10 minutes, or until the vegetables are just tender.

4 Stir the cilantro, cherry tomatoes, and shrimp into the soup and heat through for 5 minutes.

5 Transfer the soup to a warmed soup tureen or individual serving bowls and serve hot.

COOK'S TIP
Thai ginger or galangal
is a member of the ginger
family, but it is yellow in color
with pink sprouts. The flavor
is aromatic and less pungent
than ginger.

thai-style seafood soup

serves four

5 cups fish bouillon

1 lemongrass stalk, split lengthwise

pared peel of ½ lime or 1 kaffir
    lime leaf

1-inch/2.5-cm piece fresh
    gingerroot, sliced

¼ tsp chili paste

4–6 scallions

7 oz/200 g large or medium raw
    shrimp, peeled and deveined

9 oz/250 g scallops (about 16–20)

2 tbsp fresh cilantro leaves

salt

finely chopped red bell pepper or
    fresh red chile rings, to garnish

VARIATION
Substitute very small baby leeks,
slivered or thinly sliced
diagonally, for the scallions.
Include the green parts.

1 Put the bouillon in a wok or pan with the lemongrass, lime peel or lime leaf, ginger, and chili paste. Bring just to a boil, reduce the heat, cover, and let simmer for 10–15 minutes.

2 Cut the scallions in half lengthwise, then slice them crosswise very thinly. Cut the shrimp almost in half lengthwise, keeping their tails intact.

3 Strain the bouillon, return to the wok or pan, and bring to a simmer, with bubbles rising at the edges and the surface trembling. Add the scallions and cook for 2–3 minutes. Taste and season with salt, if needed, and stir in a little more chili paste, if you like.

4 Add the scallops and shrimp and poach for about 1 minute until they turn opaque and the shrimp curl.

5 Add the cilantro leaves, ladle the soup into warmed bowls, and garnish with red bell pepper or chiles.

crab & corn soup

serves four

1 tbsp corn oil

1 tsp Chinese five-spice powder

3 small carrots, cut into sticks

½ cup drained canned or frozen
    corn kernels

¾ cup peas

6 scallions, trimmed and sliced

1 fresh red chile, seeded and very
    thinly sliced

14 oz/400 g canned white crab
    meat, drained

6 oz/175 g egg noodles

7½ cups fish bouillon

3 tbsp light soy sauce

1 Add the corn oil to a preheated wok or large heavy skillet and heat it.

2 Add the Chinese five-spice powder, carrot sticks, corn kernels, peas, scallions, and red chile to the wok and cook for about 5 minutes, stirring constantly.

3 Add the crab meat to the wok or skillet and gently stir-fry the mixture over medium heat for about 1 minute, making sure that the crab meat is evenly distributed.

4 Coarsely break up the egg noodles and add to the wok or skillet.

5 Pour the fish bouillon and soy sauce into the mixture in the wok and bring to a boil.

6 Cover the wok or skillet and let simmer the soup for 5 minutes.

7 Stir once more, then ladle the soup into a warmed soup tureen or individual serving bowls and serve immediately, while piping hot.

coconut & crab soup

serves four

1 tbsp peanut oil

2 tbsp red curry paste

1 red bell pepper, seeded and sliced

2½ cups coconut milk

2½ cups fish bouillon

2 tbsp Thai fish sauce

8 oz/225 g drained canned or fresh
    white crab meat

8 oz/225 g fresh or thawed frozen
    crab claws

2 tbsp chopped fresh cilantro

3 scallions, trimmed and sliced

COOK'S TIP

Clean the wok after use by
washing it with water, using a
mild detergent if necessary, and
a soft cloth or brush. Do not
scrub or use any abrasive cleaner,
as this will scratch the surface.
Dry thoroughly, then wipe the
surface all over with a little oil
to protect the surface.

1 Heat the peanut oil in a large
preheated wok.

2 Add the red curry paste and
red bell pepper to the wok and
stir-fry for 1 minute.

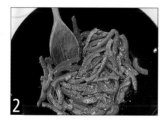

3 Add the coconut milk, fish
bouillon, and fish sauce and bring
to a boil.

4 Add the crab meat, crab claws,
chopped cilantro, and scallions
to the wok.

5 Stir the mixture well and heat
thoroughly for 2–3 minutes, or
until everything is warmed through.

6 Transfer the soup to warmed
bowls and serve hot.

chili fish soup

serves four

½ oz/15 g dried
  Chinese mushrooms

2 tbsp corn oil

1 onion, sliced

1½ cups snow peas

3½ oz/100 g canned, drained
  bamboo shoots

3 tbsp sweet chili sauce

5 cups fish or vegetable bouillon

3 tbsp light soy sauce

2 tbsp chopped fresh cilantro, plus
  extra to garnish

1 lb/450 g cod fillet, skinned
  and cubed

COOK'S TIP

There are many different varieties
of dried mushrooms, but shiitake
are best. They are quite
expensive, but a small amount
will go a long way.

1 Place the mushrooms in a
  large bowl. Pour over enough
boiling water to cover and let stand
for 5 minutes. Drain the mushrooms
thoroughly in a strainer. Using a sharp
knife, coarsely chop them.

2 Heat the corn oil in a preheated
  wok or large skillet. Add the
sliced onion to the wok and cook for
5 minutes, or until softened.

3 Add the snow peas, bamboo
  shoots, chili sauce, bouillon,
and soy sauce to the wok and bring
to a boil.

4 Add the cilantro and cod and let
  simmer for 5 minutes, or until the
fish is cooked through.

5 Transfer the soup to warmed
  bowls, garnish with extra cilantro,
if you like, and serve hot.

hot & sour mushroom soup

serves four

2 tbsp tamarind paste

4 fresh red chiles, seeded and very
finely chopped

2 garlic cloves, minced

2 tsp finely chopped Thai ginger

4 tbsp Thai fish sauce

2 tbsp palm sugar or
superfine sugar

8 kaffir lime leaves, torn coarsely

5 cups vegetable bouillon

1 large carrot, sliced thinly

8 oz/225 g white
mushrooms, halved

12 oz/350 g shredded
white cabbage

3½ oz/100 g fine green
beans, halved

3 tbsp coarsely chopped
fresh cilantro

3½ oz/100 g cherry
tomatoes, halved

1 Place the tamarind paste, red
chiles, garlic, ginger, fish sauce,
sugar, lime leaves, and vegetable
bouillon in a large preheated wok or
heavy skillet. Bring the mixture to a
boil, stirring occasionally.

2 Reduce the heat and add the
carrots, mushrooms, white
cabbage, and green beans. Let simmer,
uncovered, for 10 minutes, or until all
the vegetables are tender, but not soft.

3 Stir the fresh cilantro and cherry
tomatoes into the mixture in
the wok and heat through for an
additional 5 minutes.

4 Transfer the soup to a warmed
tureen or individual serving
bowls and serve immediately.

COOK'S TIP

Tamarind is the dried fruit of
the tamarind tree. Sold as a
pulp or paste, it is used to give
a special sweet and sour
flavor to Asian dishes.

spicy chicken noodle soup

serves four

2 tbsp tamarind paste

4 fresh red chiles, seeded and
   finely chopped

2 garlic cloves, minced

2 tsp finely chopped Thai ginger

4 tbsp Thai fish sauce

2 tbsp palm sugar or
   superfine sugar

8 kaffir lime leaves, torn coarsely

5 cups chicken bouillon

12 oz/350 g skinless, boneless
   chicken breast portions

1 large carrot, sliced thinly

2 cups diced sweet potatoes

3½ oz/100 g halved baby corn cobs

3 tbsp coarsely chopped fresh
   cilantro, plus extra to garnish

3½ oz/100 g cherry
   tomatoes, halved

5½ oz/150 g flat rice noodles

black pepper, to garnish

1 Preheat a large wok or skillet. Place the tamarind paste, chiles, garlic, ginger, fish sauce, sugar, lime leaves, and chicken bouillon in the wok and bring to a boil, stirring constantly. Reduce the heat and cook for about 5 minutes.

2 Using a sharp knife, thinly slice the chicken. Add the chicken to the wok and cook for an additional 5 minutes, stirring the mixture well.

3 Reduce the heat and add the carrots, sweet potatoes, and baby corn cobs to the wok. Let simmer, uncovered, for 5 minutes, or until the vegetables are just tender and the chicken is completely cooked through and tender.

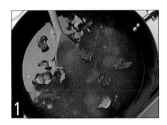

4 Stir in the chopped fresh cilantro, cherry tomatoes, and flat rice noodles.

5 Let simmer the soup for about an additional 5 minutes, or until the noodles are tender.

6 Garnish the spicy chicken noodle soup with chopped fresh cilantro and black pepper and serve hot.

eggplant & mushroom-stuffed omelet

serves four

3 tbsp vegetable oil

1 garlic clove, chopped finely

1 small onion, chopped finely

1 small eggplant, diced

½ small green bell pepper, seeded
   and chopped

1 tomato, diced

1 large dried Chinese black
   mushroom, soaked, drained,
   and sliced

1 tbsp light soy sauce

½ tsp sugar

¼ tsp pepper

2 extra large eggs

salad greens, tomato wedges, and
   cucumber slices, to garnish

1 Heat half the oil in a preheated
wok and cook the garlic over high
heat for 30 seconds. Add the onion
and eggplant and stir-fry until golden.

2 Add the green bell pepper and
stir-fry for 1 minute. Stir in the
tomato, mushroom, soy sauce, sugar,
and pepper. Remove from the wok
and keep hot.

3 Beat the eggs lightly. Heat the
remaining oil, swirling to coat the
wok. Pour in the eggs and swirl to set
around the wok. When the egg is set,
spoon the filling into the center. Fold in
the sides of the omelet to make a neat,
square package.

4 Slide the omelet carefully onto a
warmed dish and garnish with
salad greens, tomato wedges, and
cucumber slices. Serve hot.

COOK'S TIP

If you heat the wok thoroughly
before adding the oil, and heat
the oil before adding the
ingredients, they will not stick
to the wok.

thai-style spicy corn fritters

serves four

¾ cup drained canned or frozen
corn kernels

2 fresh red chiles, seeded and very
finely chopped

2 garlic cloves, minced

10 kaffir lime leaves, chopped finely

2 tbsp chopped fresh cilantro

1 extra large egg

½ cup cornmeal

3½ oz/100 g fine green beans,
sliced thinly

peanut oil

COOK'S TIP

Kaffir lime leaves are dark green,
glossy leaves that have a
lemony-lime flavor. They can be
bought from specialist Asian
stores either fresh or dried.

1 Place the corn, chiles, garlic,
lime leaves, cilantro, egg, and
cornmeal in a large mixing bowl,
and stir to mix.

2 Add the green beans to the
ingredients in the bowl and
mix well, using a wooden spoon.

3 Divide the mixture into small,
even-size balls. Flatten the balls
of mixture between the palms
of your hands to form rounds.

4 Heat a little peanut oil in a
preheated wok or large skillet
until really hot. Cook the fritters, in
batches, until brown and crisp on
the outside, turning occasionally.

5 Leave the fritters to drain on
paper towels while cooking
the remaining fritters.

6 Using a spatula, transfer the
drained fritters to warmed serving
plates and serve immediately.

vegetable spring rolls

serves four

3 small carrots

1 red bell pepper

1 tbsp corn oil, plus extra
    for cooking

¾ cup bean sprouts

finely grated peel and juice of 1 lime

1 fresh red chile, seeded and very
    finely chopped

1 tbsp light soy sauce

½ tsp arrowroot

2 tbsp chopped fresh cilantro

8 sheets phyllo pastry

2 tbsp butter

2 tsp sesame oil

TO SERVE

scallion tassels

chili sauce

1 Using a sharp knife, cut the carrots into thin sticks. Seed the bell pepper and cut into thin slices.

2 Heat the corn oil in a large preheated wok.

3 Add the carrot, red bell pepper, and bean sprouts and cook, stirring, for 2 minutes, or until softened. Remove the wok from the heat and toss in the lime peel and juice, and the red chile.

4 Mix the soy sauce with the arrowroot. Stir the mixture into the wok, return to the heat and cook for 2 minutes, until the juices thicken.

5 Add the chopped fresh cilantro to the wok and mix well, then remove the wok from the heat.

6 Lay the sheets of phyllo pastry out on a board. Melt the butter and sesame oil and brush each sheet with the mixture.

7 Spoon a little of the vegetable filling onto the top of each sheet, fold over each long side, and roll up.

8 Add a little oil to the wok and cook the spring rolls, in batches, for 2–3 minutes, or until crisp and golden brown.

9 Transfer the spring rolls to a serving dish, garnish with the scallion tassels, and serve hot with chili dipping sauce.

spicy chicken livers with bok choy

serves four

12 oz/350 g chicken livers

2 tbsp corn oil

1 fresh red chile, seeded and chopped

1 tsp grated fresh gingerroot

2 garlic cloves, minced

2 tbsp tomato catsup

3 tbsp dry sherry

3 tbsp light soy sauce

1 tsp cornstarch

1 lb/450 g bok choy

egg noodles, to serve

1 Using a sharp knife, trim the fat from the chicken livers and slice them into small pieces.

2 Heat the oil in a large preheated wok. Add the chicken liver pieces and cook for 2–3 minutes.

3 Add the chile, ginger, and garlic and cook for about 1 minute.

4 Mix the tomato catsup, sherry, soy sauce, and cornstarch in a small bowl and set aside.

5 Add the bok choy to the wok and cook until it just wilts.

6 Add the reserved tomato catsup mixture to the wok and cook, stirring to mix, until the juices are just starting to bubble.

7 Transfer to serving bowls and serve hot with noodles.

crispy seaweed

serves four

2 lb 4 oz/1 kg bok choy

3½ cups peanut oil for deep-frying

1 tsp salt

1 tbsp superfine sugar

2½ tbsp toasted pine nuts

1 Rinse the bok choy leaves under cold running water and pat dry thoroughly with paper towels.

2 Discarding any tough outer leaves, roll each bok choy leaf up, then slice through thinly so that the leaves are finely shredded. Alternatively, use a food processor to shred the bok choy.

3 Heat the peanut oil in a large preheated wok or heavy skillet.

4 Carefully add the shredded bok choy leaves to the wok or skillet and cook for about 30 seconds, or until they shrivel up and become crisp (you will probably need to do this in several batches, depending on the size of your wok).

5 Remove the crispy "seaweed" from the wok with a slotted spoon and drain on paper towels.

6 Transfer the crispy seaweed to a large bowl and toss with the salt, sugar, and pine nuts. Serve immediately on warmed serving plates.

chicken balls with dipping sauce

serves four

2 large skinless, boneless chicken
  breast portions
3 tbsp vegetable oil
2 shallots, chopped finely
½ celery stalk, chopped finely
1 garlic clove, minced
2 tbsp light soy sauce
1 egg, beaten lightly
1 bunch of scallions
salt and pepper
scallion tassels, to garnish
DIPPING SAUCE
3 tbsp dark soy sauce
1 tbsp Chinese rice wine
1 tsp sesame seeds

1 Cut the chicken into ¾-inch/2-cm pieces. Heat half of the oil in a preheated wok or skillet and stir-fry the chicken over high heat for 2–3 minutes, until golden. Remove from the wok or skillet with a slotted spoon and set aside.

2 Add the shallots, celery, and garlic to the wok or skillet and stir-fry for 1–2 minutes, until softened.

3 Place the chicken, shallots, celery, and garlic in a food processor and process until finely ground. Add 1 tablespoon of the light soy sauce and just enough egg to make a fairly firm mixture. Season to taste with salt and pepper.

4 Trim the scallions and cut into 2-inch/5-cm lengths. Make the dipping sauce by mixing together the dark soy sauce, rice wine, and sesame seeds in a small serving bowl and set aside until ready to serve.

5 Shape the chicken mixture into 16–18 walnut-size balls. Heat the remaining oil in the wok or skillet and stir-fry the chicken balls, in small batches, for 4–5 minutes, until golden brown. As each batch is cooked, drain on paper towels and keep hot.

6 Add the scallions to the wok or skillet and stir-fry for 1–2 minutes, until they start to soften, then stir in the remaining light soy sauce. Serve immediately with the chicken balls and the bowl of dipping sauce on a platter, garnished with the scallion tassels.

shrimp parcels

serves four

1 tbsp corn oil

1 red bell pepper, seeded and
    thinly sliced

¾ cup bean sprouts

finely grated peel and juice of 1 lime

1 fresh red chile, seeded and very
    finely chopped

1 tsp grated fresh gingerroot

8 oz/225 g shelled raw shrimp

1 tbsp Thai fish sauce

½ tsp arrowroot

2 tbsp chopped fresh cilantro

8 sheets phyllo pastry

2 tbsp butter

2 tsp sesame oil

3 tbsp vegetable oil

scallion tassels, to garnish

chili dipping sauce, to serve

1 Heat the corn oil in a large preheated wok. Add the red bell pepper and bean sprouts and stir-fry for 2 minutes, or until the vegetables have softened.

2 Remove the wok from the heat and toss in the lime peel and juice, red chile, ginger, and shrimp, stirring well.

3 Mix the fish sauce with the arrowroot and stir into the wok. Return the wok to the heat and cook, stirring, for 2 minutes, until the juices thicken. Toss in the cilantro and mix.

4 Lay the sheets of phyllo pastry out on a board. Melt the butter with the sesame oil and brush each pastry sheet with the mixture.

5 Spoon a little of the shrimp filling onto the top of each sheet, fold over each end, and roll up to enclose the filling.

6 Heat the oil in a large wok. Cook the parcels, in batches, for about 2–3 minutes, or until crisp and golden. Garnish with scallion tassels and serve hot with a chili dipping sauce.

crispy chili & peanut shrimp

serves four

1 lb/450 g jumbo shrimp, shelled
   leaving the tails intact
3 tbsp crunchy peanut butter
1 tbsp chili sauce
10 sheets phyllo pastry
2 tbsp butter, melted
1¾ oz/50 g fine egg noodles
oil, for cooking

1 Using a sharp knife, make a small horizontal slit across the back of each shrimp. Press down on the shrimps so they lie flat.

2 Mix the peanut butter and chili sauce in a small bowl until well blended. Using a pastry brush, spread a little of the sauce onto each shrimp so they are evenly coated.

3 Cut each pastry sheet in half and brush with melted butter.

4 Wrap each shrimp in a piece of pastry, tucking the edges under to enclose it fully.

5 Place the fine egg noodles in a bowl, pour over enough boiling water to cover, and let stand for 5 minutes, or according to the package instructions. Drain the noodles thoroughly. Use 2–3 cooked noodles to tie around each shrimp parcel.

6 Heat the oil in a preheated wok. Cook the shrimp, in batches if necessary, for 3–4 minutes, or until golden and crisp.

7 Remove the shrimp with a slotted spoon, transfer to paper towels, and drain. Transfer to serving plates and serve warm.

1

2

5

thai-style fish patties

serves four

1 lb/450 g cod fillet, skinned

2 tbsp Thai fish sauce

2 fresh red Thai chiles, seeded and
finely chopped, plus extra
to garnish

2 garlic cloves, minced

10 kaffir lime leaves, chopped finely

2 tbsp chopped fresh cilantro

1 extra large egg

¼ cup all-purpose flour

3½ oz/100 g fine green beans,
sliced thinly

peanut oil, for cooking

COOK'S TIP

Thai fish sauce is a salty, brown
liquid, which is a must for
authentic flavor. It is used
to salt dishes, but is milder
in flavor than soy sauce. It
is available from Asian food
stores or health food stores.

1 Using a sharp knife, coarsely cut
the cod into bite-size pieces.

2 Place the cod pieces in a food
processor together with the fish
sauce, chiles, garlic, lime leaves,
cilantro, egg, and all-purpose flour.
Process until finely chopped and turn
out into a large mixing bowl.

3 Add the green beans to the cod
mixture and mix.

4 Divide the mixture into small balls.
Flatten the balls between the
palms of your hands to form rounds.

5 Heat a little oil in a preheated
wok. Cook the fish patties on
both sides until brown and crisp on the
outside and cooked through.

6 Transfer the fish patties to serving
plates, garnish with fresh chiles
and serve hot.

shrimp omelet

serves four

3 tbsp corn oil

2 leeks, trimmed and sliced

12 oz/350 g shelled raw
　　jumbo shrimp

4 tbsp cornstarch

1 tsp salt

6 oz/175 g mushrooms, sliced

1¾ cups bean sprouts

6 eggs

deep-fried leeks, to
　　garnish (optional)

1 Heat the corn oil in a large preheated wok or large skillet. Add the sliced leeks and stir-fry for 3 minutes.

2 Rinse the shrimp under cold running water and pat them dry with paper towels.

3 Mix the cornstarch and salt together in a large bowl.

4 Add the shrimp to the cornstarch and salt mixture and toss to coat all over.

5 Add the shrimp to the wok or skillet and stir-fry for 2 minutes, or until the shrimp are pink and almost cooked through.

6 Add the mushrooms and bean sprouts to the wok and cook for an additional 2 minutes.

7 Beat the eggs with 3 tablespoons of cold water. Pour the egg mixture into the wok and cook until the egg sets, carefully turning over once. Turn the omelet out onto a clean board, divide into 4, and serve immediately, garnished with deep-fried leeks (if using).

sesame shrimp toasts

serves four

8 oz/225 g shelled cooked shrimp

1 scallion

¼ tsp salt

1 tsp light soy sauce

1 tbsp cornstarch

1 egg white, beaten

3 thin slices white bread,
    crusts removed

4 tbsp sesame seeds

vegetable oil, for deep-frying

COOK'S TIP

Deep-fry the triangles in
2 batches, keeping the first batch
warm while you cook the
second, to prevent them from
sticking together.

1 Put the shrimp and scallion in a food processor and process until finely ground. Alternatively, chop them very finely. Transfer to a bowl and stir in the salt, soy sauce, cornstarch, and egg white.

2 Spread the mixture onto one side of each slice of bread. Spread the sesame seeds on top of the mixture, pressing down well.

3 Cut each slice into 4 equal triangles or strips.

4 Heat the oil in a preheated wok until almost smoking. Carefully place the triangles in the oil, coated side down, and cook for 2–3 minutes, until golden brown. Remove with a slotted spoon and drain on paper towels. Serve hot.

salt & pepper shrimp

serves four

2 tsp salt

1 tsp black pepper

2 tsp Szechuan peppercorns

1 tsp sugar

1 lb/450 g shelled raw jumbo shrimp

2 tbsp peanut oil

1 fresh red chile, seeded and
    finely chopped

1 tsp freshly grated gingerroot

3 garlic cloves, minced

sliced scallions, to garnish

shrimp crackers, to serve

COOK'S TIP

Jumbo shrimp are widely
available and have a lovely
meaty texture. If using cooked
shrimp, add them with the salt
and pepper mixture in step 5—
if the cooked shrimp are added
any earlier, they will toughen
up and be inedible.

1 Grind the salt, black pepper, and Szechuan peppercorns with a pestle and mortar.

2 Mix the salt and pepper mixture with the sugar and set aside until required.

3 Rinse the jumbo shrimp under cold running water and pat dry with paper towels.

4 Heat the oil in a preheated wok or large skillet.

5 Add the shrimp, chopped red chile, ginger, and garlic to the wok or skillet and cook for 4–5 minutes, or until the shrimp are cooked through.

6 Add the salt and pepper mixture to the wok and cook for 1 minute, stirring constantly so it does not burn on the bottom of the wok.

7 Transfer the shrimp to warmed serving bowls and garnish with scallions. Serve with shrimp crackers.

vegetarian spring rolls

serves four

1 oz/25 g fine cellophane noodles

2 tbsp peanut oil

2 garlic cloves, minced

½ tsp grated fresh gingerroot

⅔ cup oyster mushrooms,
    sliced thinly

2 scallions, chopped finely

½ cup bean sprouts

1 small carrot, shredded finely

½ tsp sesame oil

1 tbsp light soy sauce

1 tbsp Chinese rice wine or dry sherry

¼ tsp pepper

1 tbsp chopped fresh cilantro

1 tbsp chopped fresh mint

24 spring-roll wrappers

½ tsp cornstarch

peanut oil, for deep-frying

fresh mint sprigs, to garnish

dipping sauce, to serve

1 Place the noodles in a heatproof bowl, pour over enough boiling water to cover, and let stand for 4 minutes. Drain, rinse in cold water, then drain again. Cut or snip into 2-inch/5-cm lengths.

2 Heat the peanut oil in a wok or wide pan over high heat. Add the garlic, fresh ginger, sliced oyster mushrooms, scallions, bean sprouts, and carrot and stir-fry for about 1 minute, until just soft.

3 Stir in the sesame oil, soy sauce, rice wine or sherry, pepper, cilantro, and mint, then remove the wok or pan from the heat. Stir in the rice noodles.

4 Arrange the spring-roll wrappers on a counter, pointing diagonally. Mix the cornstarch with 1 tablespoon water and brush the edges of 1 wrapper with this. Spoon a little filling onto the point of the wrapper.

5 Roll the point of the wrapper over the filling, then fold the side points inward over the filling. Continue to roll up the wrapper away from you, moistening the tip with more cornstarch mixture to secure to the roll.

6 Heat the oil in a preheated wok or deep pan to 375°F/190°C. Add the rolls in batches and deep-fry for 2–3 minutes each, until golden and crisp. Drain on paper towels and keep warm while you cook the remaining batches. Garnish with mint sprigs and serve hot with dipping sauce.

seven-spice eggplant

serves four

1 lb/450 g eggplant

1 egg white

3½ tbsp cornstarch

1 tbsp seven-spice seasoning

oil, for deep-frying

salt

COOK'S TIP

The best oil to use for deep-frying is peanut oil, which has a high smoke point and mild flavor, so it will neither burn nor taint the food. About 2½ cups of oil is sufficient.

---

1 Using a sharp knife, thinly slice the eggplant. Place the slices in a strainer, sprinkle with salt, and let stand for 30 minutes. This will remove all the bitter juices.

2 Rinse the eggplant slices thoroughly and pat dry with paper towels.

3 Place the egg white in a small bowl and whisk with a fork until light and foamy.

4 Using a spoon, mix the cornstarch, 1 teaspoon salt, and the seven-spice seasoning on a plate.

5 Pour the oil for deep-frying into a large preheated wok or heavy skillet and heat until very hot.

6 Dip the eggplant into the egg white, then into the cornstarch and seven-spice mixture to coat evenly.

7 Deep-fry the coated eggplant slices, in batches, for 5 minutes, or until pale golden and crisp.

8 Transfer the eggplant to paper towels and let drain. Transfer the seven-spice eggplant to serving plates and serve hot.

Poultry & Meat

Meat is expensive in Far Eastern countries and is

eaten in smaller proportions than in the Western

world. However, when meat is used, it is done

so to its full potential—it is marinated or spiced and mixed with other delicious

flavorings to create a wide array of mouthwatering dishes.

In Malaysia, a wide variety of spicy meats is offered, reflecting the many

ethnic origins of the population. In China, poultry, lamb, beef, or pork are

cooked or steamed in the wok and combined with sauces and seasonings such

as soy, black bean, and oyster sauce. In Japan, meat is usually marinated and

quickly cooked in a wok over a very high heat or simmered in miso bouillon.

Thai dishes use meat that is leaner and more flavorsome due to its

"free-range" rearing.

coconut chicken curry

serves four

2 tbsp corn oil

1 lb/450 g skinless, boneless
    chicken thighs or breast portions

1 cup okra

1 large onion, sliced

2 garlic cloves, minced

3 tbsp mild curry paste

1¼ cups chicken bouillon

1 tbsp fresh lemon juice

1¾ cup coconut cream

1¼ cups cubed fresh or
    canned pineapple

⅔ cup thick, plain yogurt

2 tbsp chopped fresh cilantro

cooked rice, to serve

TO GARNISH

lemon wedges

fresh cilantro sprigs

1 Heat the corn oil in a preheated
wok. Cut the chicken into bite-
size pieces, add to the wok, and stir-fry
until evenly browned.

2 Using a sharp knife, trim the okra.
Add the onion, garlic, and okra
to the wok and cook for an additional
2–3 minutes, stirring constantly.

3 Mix the curry paste with the
chicken bouillon and lemon juice
and pour into the wok. Bring to a boil,
cover, and let simmer for 30 minutes.

4 Stir the coconut cream into
the curry and cook for about
5 minutes.

5 Add the pineapple, yogurt, and
cilantro and cook for 2 minutes,
stirring. Garnish with lemon wedges
and cilantro and serve with cooked rice
on warmed serving plates.

stir-fried ginger chicken

serves four

2 tbsp corn oil

1 onion, sliced

2 carrots, cut into thin sticks

1 garlic clove, minced

12 oz/350 g skinless, boneless
  chicken breast portions

2 tbsp grated fresh gingerroot

1 tsp ground ginger

4 tbsp sweet sherry

1 tbsp tomato paste

1 tbsp raw brown sugar

generous ⅓ cup orange juice

1 tsp cornstarch

1 orange, peeled and segmented

snipped fresh chives, to garnish

1 Heat the oil in a large preheated wok. Add the onion, carrots, and garlic and stir-fry over high heat for 3 minutes, or until the vegetables start to soften.

2 Slice the chicken into thin strips. Add to the wok with the fresh and ground ginger. Stir-fry for 10 minutes, or until the chicken is well cooked through and golden in color.

3 Mix the sherry, tomato paste, sugar, orange juice, and cornstarch in a bowl. Stir the mixture into the wok and heat through until the mixture bubbles and the juices start to thicken.

4 Add the orange segments and carefully toss to mix.

5 Transfer the stir-fried chicken to warmed individual serving bowls and garnish with snipped fresh chives. Serve immediately.

chicken stir-fry with a trio of bell peppers

serves four

1 lb/450 g skinless, boneless
   chicken breast portions

2 tbsp corn oil

1 garlic clove, chopped finely

1 tbsp cumin seeds

1 tbsp grated fresh gingerroot

1 fresh red chile, seeded and sliced

1 red bell pepper, seeded and sliced

1 green bell pepper, seeded
   and sliced

1 yellow bell pepper, seeded
   and sliced

1 cup bean sprouts

12 oz/350 g bok choy or other
   green leaves

2 tbsp sweet chili sauce

3 tbsp light soy sauce

deep-fried gingerroot, to garnish
   (see Cook's Tip)

freshly cooked noodles, to serve

1 Using a sharp knife, slice the chicken into thin strips.

2 Heat the corn oil in a large preheated wok.

3 Add the chicken to the wok and stir–fry for 5 minutes.

4 Add the garlic, cumin seeds, gingerroot, and chile to the wok, stirring to mix.

5 Add all of the bell peppers to the wok and stir-fry for 5 minutes.

6 Toss in the bean sprouts and bok choy together with the sweet chili sauce and soy sauce and continue to stir-fry until the bok choy leaves start to wilt.

7 Transfer to serving bowls. garnish with deep-fried gingerroot (see Cook's Tip) and serve with noodles.

COOK'S TIP

To make the deep-fried gingerroot garnish, peel and thinly slice a large piece of gingerroot, using a sharp knife. Carefully lower the slices of ginger into a wok or small pan of hot oil and cook for about 30 seconds. Remove the deep-fried gingerroot with a slotted spoon, transfer to sheets of paper towels and set aside to drain thoroughly.

sweet-&-sour chicken with mango

serves four

1 tbsp corn oil

6 skinless, boneless chicken thighs

1 ripe mango

2 garlic cloves, chopped finely

8 oz/225 g leeks, shredded

1 cup bean sprouts

⅔ cup mango juice

1 tbsp white wine vinegar

2 tbsp honey

2 tbsp tomato catsup

1 tsp cornstarch

1 Heat the corn oil in a large preheated wok.

2 Using a sharp knife, cut the chicken into bite-size cubes.

3 Add the chicken to the wok and stir-fry over high heat for 10 minutes, tossing frequently, until the chicken is cooked through and golden in color.

4 Meanwhile, peel, pit, and slice the mango.

5 Add the garlic, leeks, mango, and bean sprouts to the wok and stir-fry for an additional 2–3 minutes, or until the leeks are softened.

6 Mix the mango juice, white wine vinegar, honey, and tomato catsup with the cornstarch in a measuring cup or bowl.

7 Pour the mango juice and cornstarch mixture into the wok and stir-fry for 2 minutes, or until the juices start to thicken.

8 Transfer to a warmed serving dish and serve immediately.

chicken, collards & yellow bean stir-fry

serves four

2 tbsp corn oil

1 lb/450 g skinless, boneless
   chicken breast portions

2 garlic cloves, chopped finely

1 green bell pepper

1½ cups snow peas

6 scallions, sliced, plus extra
   to garnish

8 oz/225 g collard greens or
   cabbage, shredded

5¾ oz/160 g jar yellow bean sauce

3 tbsp roasted cashew nuts

1 Heat the corn oil in a
   large preheated wok.

2 Using a sharp knife, slice the
   chicken into thin strips.

3 Add the chicken to the wok
   together with the garlic. Stir-fry
for about 5 minutes, or until the
chicken is sealed on all sides and
starting to turn golden.

4 Using a sharp knife, seed the
   green bell pepper and cut into
thin strips.

5 Add the snow peas, scallions,
   green bell pepper strips, and
collard greens or cabbage to the wok.
Stir-fry for an additional 5 minutes, or
until the vegetables are just tender.

6 Stir in the yellow bean sauce and
   heat through for about 2 minutes,
or until the mixture starts to bubble.

7 Sprinkle with the roasted
   cashews, then remove the wok
from the heat.

8 Transfer the chicken, collards, and
   yellow bean stir-fry to warmed
individual serving plates and garnish
with extra scallions, if you like. Serve
the stir-fry immediately.

chicken, bell pepper & orange stir-fry

serves four

3 tbsp corn oil

12 oz/350 g skinless, boneless
    chicken thighs, cut into thin strips

1 onion, sliced

1 garlic clove, minced

1 red bell pepper, seeded and sliced

3 oz/85 g snow peas

4 tbsp light soy sauce

4 tbsp dry sherry

1 tbsp tomato paste

finely grated peel and juice of 1 orange

1 tsp cornstarch

2 oranges

2 cups bean sprouts

cooked rice or egg noodles,
    to serve

COOK'S TIP

Bean sprouts are sprouting
mung beans and are a regular
ingredient in Chinese cooking.
They require very little cooking
and may even be eaten raw,
if you like.

1 Heat the corn oil in a large preheated wok. Add the chicken and stir-fry for 2–3 minutes, or until sealed and lightly colored on all sides.

2 Add the onion, garlic, red bell pepper, and snow peas to the wok. Stir-fry for 5 minutes, or until the vegetables are just tender and the chicken is completely cooked through.

3 Mix the soy sauce, sherry, tomato paste, orange peel and juice, and the cornstarch. Add to the wok and cook, stirring constantly, until the juices start to thicken.

4 Using a sharp knife, peel and segment the oranges. Add the segments to the wok with the bean sprouts and heat through for about 2 minutes.

5 Transfer the stir-fry to warmed individual serving plates and serve immediately with cooked rice or egg noodles.

thai red chicken with cherry tomatoes

serves four

1 tbsp corn oil

1 lb/450 g skinless, boneless
  chicken breast portions

2 garlic cloves, chopped finely

2 tbsp Thai red curry paste

2 tbsp grated fresh Thai ginger or
  gingerroot

1 tbsp tamarind paste

4 kaffir lime leaves

8 oz/225 g sweet potato

2½ cups coconut milk

8 oz/225 g cherry tomatoes, halved

3 tbsp chopped fresh cilantro

cooked jasmine or Thai fragrant rice,
  to serve

1 Heat the corn oil in a large preheated wok.

2 Thinly slice the chicken. Add the chicken to the wok and stir-fry for 5 minutes.

3 Add the garlic, curry paste, Thai ginger or gingerroot, tamarind, and lime leaves to the wok and stir-fry for 1 minute.

4 Using a sharp knife, peel and dice the sweet potato.

5 Add the coconut milk and sweet potato to the mixture in the wok and bring to a boil. Bubble over medium heat for about 20 minutes, or until the juices start to thicken and reduce slightly.

6 Add the cherry tomatoes and chopped cilantro to the curry and cook for an additional 5 minutes, stirring occasionally. Transfer the curry to warm individual serving plates and serve immediately with cooked jasmine or Thai fragrant rice.

chicken chop suey

serves four

4 tbsp light soy sauce

2 tsp brown sugar

1 lb 2 oz/500 g skinless, boneless
   chicken breasts

3 tbsp vegetable oil

2 onions, cut into fourths

2 garlic cloves, minced

3½ cups bean sprouts

3 tsp sesame oil

1 tbsp cornstarch

3 tbsp water

scant 2 cups chicken bouillon

shredded leek, to garnish

1 Mix the soy sauce and sugar together, stirring until the sugar has dissolved.

2 Trim any fat from the chicken and cut into thin strips. Place the meat in a shallow dish and spoon the soy mixture over them, turning to coat. Let marinate in the refrigerator for about 20 minutes.

3 Heat the vegetable oil in a preheated wok and cook the chicken for 2–3 minutes, until golden brown. Add the onions and garlic and cook for an additional 2 minutes. Add the bean sprouts, cook for 4–5 minutes, then add the sesame oil.

4 Mix the cornstarch and water to form a smooth paste. Pour the bouillon into the wok, add the cornstarch paste and bring to a boil, stirring until the sauce is thickened. Serve, garnished with shredded leek, on warmed serving plates.

yellow bean chicken

serves four

1 lb/450 g skinless, boneless
chicken breast portions

1 egg white, beaten

1 tbsp cornstarch

1 tbsp rice wine vinegar

1 tbsp light soy sauce

1 tsp superfine sugar

3 tbsp vegetable oil

1 garlic clove, minced

½-inch/1-cm piece fresh
gingerroot, grated

1 green bell pepper, seeded
and diced

2 large mushrooms, sliced

3 tbsp yellow bean sauce

yellow or green bell pepper strips,
to garnish

VARIATION

Black bean sauce would
work equally well with this
recipe. Although this would
affect the appearance of the
dish, because black bean
sauce is much darker, the
flavors would be compatible.

---

1 Trim any fat from the chicken and cut the meat into 1-inch/2.5-cm cubes.

2 Mix the egg white and cornstarch in a shallow bowl. Add the chicken and turn in the mixture to coat. Set aside for 20 minutes.

3 Mix the rice wine vinegar, soy sauce, and superfine sugar in a small bowl.

4 Remove the chicken from the egg white mixture.

5 Heat the oil in a preheated wok, add the chicken, and stir-fry for 3–4 minutes, until golden brown all over. Remove the chicken from the wok with a slotted spoon, drain on paper towels, and keep warm.

6 Add the garlic, ginger, bell pepper, and mushrooms to the wok and stir-fry for 1–2 minutes.

7 Add the yellow bean sauce and cook for 1 minute. Stir in the vinegar mixture and return the chicken to the wok. Cook for 1–2 minutes and serve, garnished with bell pepper.

chicken & peas

serves four

1 cup dried black-eyed peas, soaked
    overnight and drained

1 tsp salt

2 onions, chopped

2 garlic cloves, minced

1 tsp ground turmeric

1 tsp ground cumin

2 lb 12 oz/1.25 kg chicken, cut into
    8 pieces

1 green bell pepper, seeded
    and chopped

2 tbsp vegetable oil

1-inch/2.5-cm piece fresh
    gingerroot, grated

2 tsp coriander seeds

½ tsp fennel seeds

2 tsp garam masala

1 tbsp chopped fresh cilantro,
    to garnish

1 Put the dried black-eyed peas into a wok or pan with the salt, onions, garlic, turmeric, and cumin. Cover the peas with water, bring to a boil, and cook for 15 minutes.

2 Add the chicken and green bell pepper to the wok and bring to a boil. Reduce the heat and let simmer for 30 minutes, until the peas are tender and the chicken juices run clear when the thickest parts of the pieces are pierced with the point of a sharp knife.

3 Heat the vegetable oil in a wok or pan and stir-fry the grated gingerroot, coriander seeds, and fennel seeds for 30 seconds.

4 Stir the fried spices into the chicken and add the garam masala. Let simmer for an additional 5 minutes, garnish with chopped cilantro, and serve immediately.

braised garlic chicken

serves four

4 garlic cloves, chopped

4 shallots, chopped

2 small fresh red chiles, seeded
   and chopped

1 lemongrass stalk, chopped finely

1 tbsp chopped fresh cilantro

1 tsp shrimp paste

½ tsp ground cinnamon

1 tbsp tamarind paste

2 tbsp vegetable oil

8 chicken pieces, such as drumsticks
   or thighs

1¼ cups chicken bouillon

1 tbsp Thai fish sauce

1 tbsp smooth peanut butter

4 tbsp toasted peanuts, chopped

salt and pepper

TO SERVE

stir-fried vegetables

freshly cooked noodles

1 Place the garlic, shallots, chiles, lemongrass, cilantro, and shrimp paste in a mortar and grind with a pestle to an almost smooth paste. Stir in the cinnamon and tamarind paste.

2 Heat the oil in a preheated wok or skillet. Add the chicken and cook, turning frequently, until golden on all sides. Remove with a slotted spoon and keep hot. Tip away any excess fat.

3 Add the garlic paste to the wok or skillet and cook over medium heat, stirring constantly, until lightly browned. Stir in the bouillon and return the chicken to the wok or skillet.

4 Bring to a boil, then cover tightly, reduce the heat, and let simmer, stirring occasionally, for 25–30 minutes, until the chicken is tender and thoroughly cooked. Stir in the fish sauce and peanut butter and let simmer the mixture gently for about an additional 10 minutes.

5 Season with salt and pepper to taste and sprinkle the toasted peanuts over the chicken. Serve immediately, with a colorful selection of stir-fried vegetables and freshly cooked noodles.

chicken with lemon & sesame seeds

serves four

4 skinless, boneless chicken
   breast portions

1 egg white

2 tbsp sesame seeds

2 tbsp vegetable oil

1 onion, sliced

1 tbsp raw brown sugar

finely grated peel and juice of
   1 lemon

3 tbsp lemon curd

7 oz/200 g canned water chestnuts

strips of lemon peel, to garnish

freshly cooked rice, to serve

COOK'S TIP

Water chestnuts are
commonly added to Chinese
recipes for their crunchy
texture, as they do not have a
great deal of flavor.

---

1 Place the chicken portions between 2 sheets of plastic wrap and pound with a rolling pin to flatten. Slice the chicken into thin strips.

2 Whisk the egg white until light and foamy.

3 Dip the chicken strips into the egg white, then into the sesame seeds until coated evenly.

4 Heat the vegetable oil in a large preheated wok.

5 Add the onion slices to the wok and stir-fry for 2 minutes, or until just softened.

6 Add the sesame-coated chicken to the wok and continue stir-frying for 5 minutes, or until golden.

7 Mix the sugar, lemon peel, lemon juice, and the lemon curd together, and add the mixture to the wok. Let the lemon mixture bubble slightly without stirring.

8 Drain and rinse the water chestnuts and slice them thinly, using a sharp knife. Add the water chestnuts to the wok and heat through for 2 minutes. Transfer to serving bowls, garnish with lemon peel, and serve hot with rice.

chicken with cashews & yellow bean sauce

serves four

1 lb/450 g boneless chicken
  breast portions

2 tbsp vegetable oil

1 red onion, sliced

1½ cups sliced flat mushrooms

⅓ cup cashew nuts

2¾ oz/75 g jar yellow bean sauce

fresh cilantro, to garnish

egg fried rice, to serve

COOK'S TIP

Boneless chicken thighs could
be used instead for a more
economical dish.

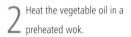

1 Using a sharp knife, remove
the excess skin from the chicken if
you like. Cut the chicken into small,
bite-size chunks.

2 Heat the vegetable oil in a
preheated wok.

3 Add the chunks of chicken to the
wok and stir-fry over medium
heat for 5 minutes.

4 Add the red onion and mushrooms
to the wok and continue to stir-fry
for an additional 5 minutes.

5 Place the cashew nuts on a
cookie sheet and toast under a
preheated medium broiler until just
browning—this brings out their flavor.

6 Toss the toasted cashew nuts into
the wok together with the yellow
bean sauce. Bubble the sauce, without
stirring, for 2–3 minutes.

7 Transfer the stir-fry to warmed
serving bowls and garnish with
fresh cilantro. Serve immediately with
egg fried rice.

peppered chicken with sugar snap peas

serves four

2 tbsp tomato catsup

2 tbsp light soy sauce

1 lb/450 g skinless, boneless
   chicken breast portions

2 tbsp mixed peppercorns, crushed

2 tbsp corn oil

1 red bell pepper

1 green bell pepper

2½ cups sugar snap peas

2 tbsp oyster sauce

VARIATION
Use snow peas instead of sugar
snap peas, if you like.

1 Mix the tomato catsup with the soy sauce in a bowl.

2 Using a sharp knife, slice the chicken into thin strips. Toss the chicken in the tomato catsup and soy sauce mixture.

3 Sprinkle the crushed peppercorns onto a plate. Dip the coated chicken in the peppercorns until evenly coated.

4 Heat the corn oil in a large preheated wok.

5 Add the chicken to the wok and stir-fry over medium heat for 5 minutes.

6 Seed and slice the red and green bell peppers into strips.

7 Add the bell pepper strips to the wok together with the sugar snap peas and stir-fry for 5 minutes.

8 Add the oyster sauce and bubble the mixture, without stirring, for 2 minutes. Transfer to serving bowls and serve immediately.

honey & soy chicken with bean sprouts

serves four

2 tbsp honey

3 tbsp light soy sauce

1 tsp Chinese five-spice powder

1 tbsp sweet sherry

1 garlic clove, chopped finely

8 chicken thighs

1 tbsp corn oil

1 fresh red chile

1¼ cups baby corn cobs, halved

8 scallions, sliced

1½ cups bean sprouts

COOK'S TIP

Chinese five-spice

powder is found in most

large stores and is a blend

of aromatic spices.

1 Mix the honey, soy sauce, Chinese five-spice powder, sherry, and garlic in a large bowl.

2 Using a sharp knife, make 3 slashes in the skin of each chicken thigh. Brush the honey and soy marinade all over the chicken thighs, cover with plastic wrap, and let stand for at least 30 minutes.

3 Heat the corn oil in a large preheated wok.

4 Add the chicken to the wok and cook over a fairly high heat, turning frequently, for 12–15 minutes, or until the chicken browns and the skin start to crisp. Remove the chicken with a slotted spoon.

5 Using a sharp knife, seed and very finely chop the chile.

6 Add the chile, corn, scallions, and bean sprouts to the wok and stir-fry for 5 minutes.

7 Return the chicken to the wok and briefly mix all of the ingredients together until completely heated through. Serve immediately.

stir-fried chicken with chili & crisp basil

serves four

8 chicken drumsticks

2 tbsp soy sauce

1 tbsp corn oil

1 fresh red chile

1 large carrot, cut into thin sticks

6 celery stalks, cut into sticks

3 tbsp sweet chili sauce

oil, for cooking

about 50 fresh basil leaves

freshly cooked noodles, to serve

1 Remove the skin from the chicken drumsticks, if you like. Make 3 slashes in each drumstick. Brush the drumsticks with the soy sauce.

2 Heat the corn oil in a preheated wok and cook the drumsticks for 20 minutes, turning frequently, until they are cooked through and golden.

3 Seed and finely chop the fresh chile. Add the chile, carrot, and celery to the wok and stir-fry for 5 minutes. Stir in the chili sauce, cover and bubble gently while preparing the basil leaves.

4 Heat a little oil in a heavy skillet. Carefully add the basil leaves— stand well away from the skillet and protect your hand with a dish towel, as they may spit. Cook the basil leaves for about 30 seconds, or until they begin to curl up but not brown. Drain the leaves on paper towels.

5 Transfer the cooked chicken, vegetables, and pan juices to a warmed serving platter, garnish with the deep-fried crisp basil leaves, and serve with freshly cooked noodles.

garlic chicken with cilantro & lime

serves four

4 large skinless, boneless chicken
   breast portions

3 tbsp garlic butter, softened

3 tbsp chopped fresh cilantro,
   plus extra to garnish (optional)

1 tbsp corn oil

finely grated peel and juice of
   2 limes

4 tbsp palm sugar or raw
   brown sugar

cooked rice, to serve

1 Place each chicken breast portion between 2 sheets of plastic wrap and pound with a rolling pin until flattened to ½-inch/1-cm thick.

2 Mix the garlic butter and cilantro and spread over each flattened chicken piece. Roll up, like a jelly roll, and secure with a toothpick.

3 Heat the corn oil in a preheated wok. Add the chicken rolls and cook, turning frequently, for 15–20 minutes until cooked through.

4 Remove the chicken from the wok and transfer to a board. Cut each chicken roll into slices.

5 Add the lime peel, lime juice, and sugar to the wok and heat gently, stirring constantly, until the sugar has dissolved. Raise the heat and let bubble for 2 minutes.

6 Arrange the chicken on warmed serving plates and spoon the pan juices over to serve.

7 Garnish with extra cilantro, if you like, and serve with cooked rice.

thai stir-fried chicken

serves four

3 tbsp peanut oil

12 oz/350 g skinless, boneless
   chicken breast portions, sliced

8 shallots, sliced

2 garlic cloves, chopped finely

2 tsp grated fresh gingerroot

1 fresh green chile, seeded and
   finely chopped

1 red bell pepper, seeded and
   thinly sliced

1 green bell pepper, seeded and
   thinly sliced

3 zucchini, sliced thinly

2 tbsp ground almonds

1 tsp ground cinnamon

1 tbsp oyster sauce

⅓ cup coconut cream

salt and pepper

1 Heat the peanut oil in a
preheated wok or heavy skillet.
Add the chicken, season with salt
and pepper to taste, and stir-fry over
medium heat for about 4 minutes, until
lightly colored.

2 Add the shallots, garlic, ginger,
and green chile and stir-fry for an
additional 2 minutes.

3 Add the red and green bell
peppers and zucchini and stir-fry
for about 1 minute.

4 Stir in the almonds, cinnamon,
oyster sauce, and coconut cream
and season to taste with salt and
pepper. Stir-fry for 1 minute to heat
through, then serve immediately.

COOK'S TIP
Although it is widely believed
that the seeds are the hottest
part of the chile, they do not
contain any capsaicin—the heat
factor—but it is concentrated in
the flesh surrounding them.

chicken & corn sauté

serves four

4 skinless, boneless chicken
breast portions

9 oz/250 g baby corn cobs

9 oz/250 g snow peas

2 tbsp corn oil

1 tbsp sherry vinegar

1 tbsp honey

1 tbsp light soy sauce

1 tbsp sunflower seeds

pepper

cooked rice or egg noodles, to serve

VARIATION

Rice vinegar or balsamic vinegar
make good substitutes for the
sherry vinegar.

---

1 Using a sharp knife, slice the
chicken breast portions into long,
thin strips.

2 Cut the baby corn cobs in half
lengthwise or slice diagonally.
Trim the snow peas.

3 Heat the corn oil in a preheated
wok or a wide skillet.

4 Add the strips of chicken and
stir-fry over a fairly high heat for
1 minute.

5 Add the baby corn cobs and
snow peas and stir-fry over
medium heat for 5–8 minutes, until
evenly cooked. The vegetables should
be tender, but still slightly crunchy.

6 Mix the sherry vinegar, honey,
and light soy sauce together in a
small bowl.

7 Stir the vinegar and honey
mixture into the wok or skillet
with the sunflower seeds.

8 Season with pepper to taste.
Cook, stirring, for 1 minute.

9 Serve the chicken and corn sauté
immediately with cooked rice or
egg noodles.

thai-spiced cilantro chicken

serves four

4 skinless, boneless chicken
   breast portions

2 garlic cloves, peeled

1 fresh green chile, seeded

¾-inch/2-cm piece fresh gingerroot

4 tbsp chopped fresh cilantro

finely grated peel of 1 lime

3 tbsp lime juice

2 tbsp light soy sauce

1 tbsp superfine sugar

¾ cup coconut milk

TO SERVE

plain boiled rice

cucumber and radish salad

1 Using a sharp knife, cut 3 deep slashes into the skinned side of each chicken breast portion. Place them in a single layer in a wide, nonmetallic dish.

2 Put the garlic, chile, ginger, cilantro, lime peel and juice, soy sauce, superfine sugar, and coconut milk in a food processor and process to a smooth purée.

3 Spread the purée over both sides of the chicken portions, coating them evenly. Cover the dish with

plastic wrap and let marinate in the refrigerator for about 1 hour.

4 Lift the chicken from the marinade, drain off the excess, and place in a broiler pan. Cook under a preheated broiler for 12–15 minutes, until thoroughly and evenly cooked.

5 Meanwhile, place the remaining marinade in a wok or pan and bring to a boil. Reduce the heat and let simmer for 3–5 minutes to heat thoroughly. Remove the wok or pan from the heat.

6 Place the chicken breast portions on warmed individual serving plates and pour the sauce over them. Serve immediately accompanied with plain boiled rice and cucumber and radish salad.

chicken & mango stir-fry

serves four

6 skinless, boneless chicken thighs

2 tsp grated fresh gingerroot

1 garlic clove, minced

1 small fresh red chile, seeded

1 large red bell pepper, seeded

4 scallions

scant 3 cups snow peas

scant 1 cup baby corn cobs

1 large ripe mango

2 tbsp corn oil

1 tbsp light soy sauce

3 tbsp Chinese rice wine or
dry sherry

1 tsp sesame oil

salt and pepper

snipped fresh chives, to garnish

1 Cut the chicken into long, thin strips and place in a bowl. Mix the ginger, garlic, and chile, then stir the mixture into the chicken strips to coat them evenly.

2 Slice the bell pepper thinly, cutting diagonally. Trim and diagonally slice the scallions. Cut the snow peas and corn cobs in half diagonally. Peel the mango, remove the pit, and cut into small chunks.

3 Heat the corn oil in a large, preheated wok or heavy skillet over high heat. Add the chicken and stir-fry for 4–5 minutes, until just turning golden brown. Add the bell pepper slices and stir-fry over medium heat for 4–5 minutes, until softened.

4 Add the sliced scallions, snow peas, and baby corn cobs and stir-fry for 1 minute.

5 Mix the soy sauce, rice wine or sherry, and sesame oil together, and stir the mixture into the wok. Add the mango slices and stir gently for 1 minute, until heated through.

6 Season to taste with salt and pepper, garnish with snipped fresh chives, and serve the chicken and mango stir-fry immediately.

duck with baby corn cobs & pineapple

serves four

4 duck breasts

1 tsp Chinese five-spice powder

1 tbsp cornstarch

1 tbsp chili oil

8 oz/225 g pearl onions, peeled

2 garlic cloves, minced

scant 1 cup baby corn cobs

1¼ cups canned pineapple chunks

6 scallions, sliced

1 cup bean sprouts

2 tbsp plum sauce

1 Remove any skin from the duck breasts. Cut the duck into thin slices.

2 Mix the Chinese five-spice powder and the cornstarch. Toss the duck in the mixture until well coated.

3 Heat the chili oil in a preheated wok. Add the slices of duck and stir-fry for about 10 minutes, or until just starting to crispen around the edges. Remove from the wok with a slotted spoon and keep warm.

4 Add the onions and garlic to the wok and stir-fry for 5 minutes, or until softened. Add the corn cobs and stir-fry for an additional 5 minutes. Add the pineapple, scallions, and bean sprouts and stir-fry for 3–4 minutes. Stir in the plum sauce.

5 Return the cooked duck to the wok and toss until well mixed. Transfer to warmed serving dishes and serve.

ginger duck with rice

serves four

2 duck breasts, cut diagonally into
  thin slices

2–3 tbsp Japanese soy sauce

1 tbsp mirin or medium sherry

2 tsp brown sugar

2-inch/5-cm piece fresh gingerroot,
  finely chopped or grated

4 tbsp peanut oil

2 garlic cloves, minced

1½ cups long-grain white or
  brown rice

4 cups chicken bouillon

4 oz/115 g cooked lean cured ham,
  sliced thinly

2¼ cups snow peas, cut diagonally
  in half

¾ cup bean sprouts, rinsed

8 scallions, thinly sliced diagonally

2–3 tbsp chopped fresh cilantro

sweet or hot chili sauce (optional)

2 Heat 2–3 tablespoons peanut oil in a large heavy skillet over medium-high heat. Add the garlic and half the remaining ginger and stir-fry for about 1 minute, until fragrant. Add the rice and cook, stirring, for about 3 minutes, until translucent and starting to color.

3 Add 3 cups bouillon and 1 teaspoon of soy sauce and bring to a boil. Reduce the heat to low, cover, and let simmer for 20 minutes, until the rice is tender and the liquid is absorbed. Do not uncover, but remove from the heat and set aside.

4 Heat the remaining peanut oil in a large wok. Drain the duck and gently stir-fry for about 3 minutes, until just colored. Add 1 tablespoon soy sauce and the remaining sugar and cook for 1 minute. Remove from the wok, set aside, and keep warm.

5 Stir in the ham, snow peas, bean sprouts, scallions, the remaining ginger, and half the cilantro. Add about ½ cup of the bouillon and stir-fry for 1 minute, or until the bouillon is almost completely reduced. Fork in the rice and toss together. Add a dash of chili sauce (if using).

6 Turn into a warmed serving dish, arrange the duck on top, sprinkle with the remaining cilantro, and serve.

1 Put the duck in a shallow bowl with 1 tablespoon of the soy sauce, the mirin, half the brown sugar, and one-third of the ginger. Stir to coat all over and set aside to marinate at room temperature.

duck with mangoes

serves four

2 ripe mangoes

1¼ cups chicken bouillon

2 garlic cloves, minced

1 tsp grated fresh gingerroot

2 large skinless duck breasts, about
    8 oz/225 g each

3 tbsp vegetable oil

1 tsp wine vinegar

1 tsp light soy sauce

1 leek, sliced

chopped fresh parsley, to garnish

1 Peel the mangoes and cut the flesh from each side of the pits. Cut the flesh into strips.

2 Put half of the mango pieces and the chicken bouillon in a food processor and process until smooth. Alternatively, press half of the mangoes through a fine strainer and mix with the bouillon.

3 Rub the garlic and ginger over the duck breasts. Heat the vegetable oil in a preheated wok and cook the duck breasts, turning frequently, until sealed. Set aside the oil in the wok and remove the duck.

4 Place the duck breasts on a rack set over a roasting pan and cook in a preheated oven, 425°F/220°C, for about 20 minutes, until the duck is cooked through and tender.

5 Place the mango and bouillon mixture in a small pan and add the wine vinegar and soy sauce.

6 Bring the mixture to a boil and cook over high heat, stirring constantly, until reduced by half.

7 Heat the oil reserved in the wok and stir-fry the sliced leek and remaining mango for 1 minute. Remove from the wok, transfer to a serving dish, and keep warm until ready to serve.

8 Slice the cooked duck breasts neatly and arrange the slices on top of the leek and mango mixture. Pour the sauce over the duck slices, garnish with chopped parsley, and serve immediately.

crispy duck with noodles & tamarind

serves four

3 duck breasts, total weight about
   14 oz/400 g

2 garlic cloves, minced

1½ tsp chili paste

1 tbsp honey

3 tbsp dark soy sauce

½ tsp Chinese five-spice powder

9 oz/250 g rice stick noodles

1 tsp vegetable oil

1 tsp sesame oil

2 scallions, sliced

scant 1½ cup snow peas

2 tbsp tamarind juice

sesame seeds, to garnish

1 Prick the skin of the duck breasts all over with a fork and place in a deep dish.

2 Mix the garlic, chili paste, honey, soy sauce, and Chinese five-spice powder, then pour over the duck. Turn the duck over to coat it evenly, then cover with plastic wrap, and let marinate in the refrigerator for at least 1 hour.

3 Meanwhile, soak the rice stick noodles in hot water for 15 minutes, or according to the package instructions. Drain well.

4 Drain the duck from the marinade and broil on a rack under high heat for about 10 minutes, turning it over occasionally, until it becomes a rich golden brown. Remove and slice the meat thinly.

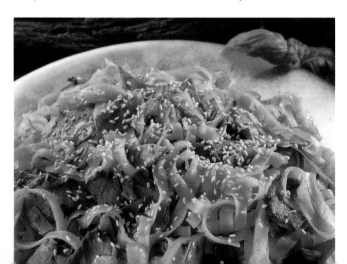

5 Heat the vegetable and sesame oils in a preheated wok and stir-fry the scallions and snow peas for 2 minutes. Stir in the marinade and tamarind juice. Bring to a boil.

6 Add the sliced duck and noodles and toss to heat thoroughly. Transfer to warmed serving plates and serve immediately, sprinkled with sesame seeds.

hoisin duck with leek & stir-fried cabbage

serves four

4 duck breasts

12 oz/350 g green cabbage

8 oz/225 g leeks, sliced

finely grated peel of 1 orange

6 tbsp oyster sauce

1 tsp toasted sesame seeds,
   to serve

1 Heat a large wok and dry-fry the duck breasts, with the skin on, for about 5 minutes on each side (you may need to do this in batches).

2 Remove the duck breasts from the wok with a slotted spoon and transfer to a clean board.

3 Using a sharp knife, cut the duck breasts into thin slices.

4 Remove and discard all but 1 tablespoon of the fat from the duck left in the wok.

5 Using a sharp knife, finely shred the green cabbage.

6 Add the leeks, green cabbage, and orange peel to the wok and cook for about 5 minutes, or until the vegetables have softened.

7 Return the duck to the wok and heat through for 2–3 minutes.

8 Drizzle the oyster sauce over the mixture in the wok, toss well until all the ingredients are mixed, then heat through.

9 Sprinkle the stir-fry with toasted sesame seeds, transfer to a warmed serving dish, and serve hot.

stir-fried turkey with cranberry glaze

serves four

1 lb/450 g boneless turkey breast

2 tbsp corn oil

2 tbsp preserved ginger

½ cup fresh or frozen cranberries

3½ oz/100 g canned chestnuts

4 tbsp cranberry sauce

3 tbsp light soy sauce

salt and pepper

COOK'S TIP

It is very important that the wok is very hot before you cook. Test by by holding your hand flat about 3 inches/7.5 cm above the base of the interior—you should be able to feel the heat radiating from it.

1 Remove any skin from the turkey breast. Using a sharp knife, thinly slice the turkey breast.

2 Heat the corn oil in a large preheated wok or heavy skillet.

3 Add the slices of turkey to the wok or skillet and stir-fry over medium heat for about 5 minutes, or until cooked through.

4 Drain the preserved ginger in a small strainer, then, using a sharp knife, chop finely.

5 Add the preserved ginger and the cranberries to the wok or skillet and cook for 2–3 minutes, or until the cranberries have started to become soft.

6 Add the chestnuts, cranberry sauce, and soy sauce, season to taste with salt and pepper, and bubble for 2–3 minutes.

7 Transfer the glazed turkey stir-fry to warmed individual serving dishes and serve immediately.

beef with bamboo shoots & snow peas

serves four

12 oz/350 g round steak

3 tbsp dark soy sauce

1 tbsp tomato catsup

2 garlic cloves, minced

1 tbsp fresh lemon juice

1 tsp ground coriander

2 tbsp vegetable oil

6 oz/175 g snow peas

7 oz/200 g canned bamboo shoots,
   drained and rinsed

1 tsp sesame oil

1 Thinly slice the meat and place in a non-metallic dish together with the dark soy sauce, tomato catsup, garlic, lemon juice, and ground coriander. Mix well so that all of the meat is coated in the marinade, cover, and let stand for at least 1 hour.

2 Heat the vegetable oil in a preheated wok. Drain the slices of meat, add to the wok, and cook for 2–4 minutes (depending on how well cooked you like your meat), or until cooked through.

3 Add the snow peas and bamboo shoots to the mixture in the wok and cook over high heat, tossing frequently, for an additional 5 minutes.

4 Drizzle with the sesame oil and toss well to mix. Transfer to serving dishes and serve hot.

chili beef stir-fry salad

serves four

1 lb/450 g lean round steak

2 garlic cloves, minced

1 tsp chili powder

½ tsp salt

1 tsp ground coriander

1 ripe avocado

2 tbsp corn oil

15 oz/425 g canned red kidney
  beans, drained

6 oz/175 g cherry tomatoes, halved

1 large package tortilla chips

shredded iceberg lettuce

chopped fresh cilantro, to serve

1 Using a sharp knife, slice the beef into thin strips.

2 Place the garlic, chili powder, salt, and ground coriander in a large bowl and mix until well blended.

3 Add the strips of beef to the marinade and toss well to coat all over.

4 Using a sharp knife, peel the avocado. Slice the avocado lengthwise, remove and discard the pit, then slice the flesh crosswise to form small dice.

5 Heat the oil in a large preheated wok. Add the beef and stir-fry for 5 minutes, tossing frequently.

6 Add the kidney beans, tomatoes, and avocado and heat through for 2 minutes.

7 Arrange a bed of tortilla chips and lettuce around the edge of a large platter and spoon the beef mixture into the center. Alternatively, serve the tortilla chips and lettuce separately.

8 Garnish with chopped fresh cilantro and serve immediately.

beef & beans

serves four

1 lb/450 g beef fillet steak or rump

   steak, cut into 1-inch/

   2.5-cm pieces

MARINADE

2 tsp cornstarch

2 tbsp dark soy sauce

2 tsp peanut oil

SAUCE

2 tbsp vegetable oil

3 garlic cloves, minced

1 small onion, cut into 8 pieces

8 oz/225 g fine green beans, halved

¼ cup unsalted cashews

1 oz/25 g canned bamboo

   shoots, drained

2 tsp dark soy sauce

2 tsp Chinese rice wine or dry sherry

½ cup beef bouillon

2 tsp cornstarch

4 tsp water

salt and pepper

1 To make the marinade, mix together thoroughly the cornstarch, soy sauce, and peanut oil.

2 Place the steak in a shallow glass bowl. Pour the marinade over the steak, turn to coat thoroughly, cover and let marinate in the refrigerator for at least 30 minutes—the longer the better.

3 To make the sauce, heat the oil in a preheated wok. Add the garlic, onion, beans, cashews, and bamboo shoots, and cook for 2–3 minutes.

4 Remove the steak from the marinade, drain, add to the wok, and cook for 3–4 minutes.

5 Mix the soy sauce, Chinese rice wine or sherry, and beef bouillon together. Blend the cornstarch with the water, then add to the soy sauce mixture. Mix well to combine.

6 Stir the mixture into the wok and bring the sauce to a boil, stirring until thickened. Reduce the heat and let simmer for 2–3 minutes. Season to taste with salt and pepper and serve immediately.

beef & vegetables with sherry & soy sauce

serves four

2 tbsp corn oil

12 oz/350 g beef tenderloin, sliced

1 red onion, sliced

6 oz/175 g zucchini

2 carrots, sliced thinly

1 red bell pepper, seeded and sliced

1 small head Napa
 cabbage, shredded

1½ cups bean sprouts

8 oz/225 g canned bamboo shoots,
 drained and rinsed

1½ cups cashew nuts, toasted

SAUCE

3 tbsp medium sherry

3 tbsp light soy sauce

1 tsp ground ginger

1 garlic clove, minced

1 tsp cornstarch

1 tbsp tomato paste

1 Heat the corn oil in a large preheated wok. Add the sliced beef and red onion to the wok and cook for about 4–5 minutes, or until the onion starts to soften and the meat is just browning.

2 Trim the zucchini and thinly slice on the diagonal.

3 Add the carrots, bell pepper, and zucchini to the wok and stir-fry the mixture for 5 minutes.

4 Toss in the Napa cabbage, bean sprouts, and bamboo shoots and heat through for 2–3 minutes, or until the leaves are just starting to wilt.

5 Sprinkle the cashews over the stir-fry and toss well to mix.

6 To make the sauce, mix the sherry, soy sauce, ground ginger, garlic, cornstarch, and tomato paste until well blended.

7 Pour the sauce over the stir-fry and toss to mix. Bubble the sauce for 2–3 minutes, or until the juices thicken and reduce slightly.

8 Transfer to warmed serving dishes and serve immediately.

beef & bell peppers with lemongrass

serves four

1 lb 2 oz/500 g lean beef tenderloin

2 tbsp vegetable oil

1 garlic clove, chopped finely

1 lemongrass stalk, shredded finely

2 tsp finely chopped fresh
   gingerroot

1 red bell pepper, seeded and
   thickly sliced

1 green bell pepper, seeded and
   thickly sliced

1 onion, sliced thickly

2 tbsp lime juice

salt and pepper

cooked noodles or rice, to serve

1 If you have time, place the beef in the freezer for 30 minutes beforehand. This helps to firm it up, which makes it easier to slice very thinly. Cut the beef into long, thin strips, cutting across the grain.

2 Heat the vegetable oil in a preheated wok or large skillet. Add the garlic and stir-fry for 1 minute.

3 Add the beef and stir-fry for an additional 2–3 minutes, until lightly colored. Stir in the lemongrass and ginger, then remove the wok or skillet from the heat.

4 Using a slotted spoon, remove the beef from the wok or skillet and keep warm. Add the bell peppers and onion to the wok or skillet and stir-fry over high heat for 2–3 minutes, until the onion is just turning golden brown and slightly softened.

5 Return the beef to the wok or skillet, stir in the lime juice, and season to taste with salt and pepper. Serve immediately with noodles or rice.

garlic beef with sesame seeds & soy sauce

serves four

2 tbsp sesame seeds

1 lb/450 g beef tenderloin

2 tbsp vegetable oil

1 green bell pepper, seeded and
thinly sliced

4 garlic cloves, minced

2 tbsp dry sherry

4 tbsp soy sauce

6 scallions, sliced

cooked noodles, to serve

COOK'S TIP
You can spread the sesame
seeds out on a cookie sheet and
toast them under a preheated
broiler until browned all over,
if you like.

1 Preheat a large wok or large,
heavy skillet over low heat until it
is very hot.

2 Add the sesame seeds to the wok
or skillet and dry-fry, stirring
constantly, for 1–2 minutes, or until
they just start to brown. Remove the
sesame seeds from the wok and set
aside until required.

3 Using a sharp knife or meat
cleaver, thinly slice the beef.

4 Heat the vegetable oil in the
wok or skillet. Add the beef and
stir-fry for 2–3 minutes, or until sealed
on all sides.

5 Add the sliced bell pepper and
minced garlic and continue
cooking for 2 minutes.

6 Add the dry sherry and soy
sauce together with the scallions.
Let the mixture in the wok or skillet
bubble, stirring occasionally, for about
1 minute, but do not let it burn.

7 Transfer the garlic beef stir-fry to
warmed serving bowls and
sprinkle with the dry-fried sesame
seeds. Serve hot with noodles.

stir-fried beef with bean sprouts

serves four

bunch of scallions, thinly
    sliced lengthwise

2 tbsp corn oil

1 garlic clove, minced

1 tsp finely chopped fresh
    gingerroot

1 lb 2 oz/500 g tender beef
    tenderloin, cut into thin strips

1 large red bell pepper, seeded
    and sliced

1 small fresh red chile, seeded
    and chopped

6 cups bean sprouts

1 small lemongrass stalk,
    chopped finely

2 tbsp smooth peanut butter

4 tbsp coconut milk

1 tbsp rice vinegar

1 tbsp soy sauce

1 tsp brown sugar

9 oz/250 g medium egg noodles

salt and pepper

1 Set aside some of the sliced
scallions for the garnish. Heat the
corn oil in a preheated wok or skillet
over high heat. Add the remaining
scallions, the garlic, and ginger and
stir-fry for 2–3 minutes, until softened.

Add the strips of beef and stir-fry for
4–5 minutes, until they are sealed and
evenly browned.

2 Add the red bell pepper and
stir-fry for an additional
3–4 minutes. Add the chile and bean
sprouts and stir-fry for 2 minutes. Mix
the lemongrass, peanut butter, coconut
milk, vinegar, soy sauce, and sugar,
then stir the mixture into the wok.

3 Meanwhile, cook the egg noodles
in lightly salted boiling water for
4 minutes, or according to the package
instructions. Drain and stir into the wok
or skillet, tossing to mix evenly.

4 Season to taste with salt and
pepper. Sprinkle the reserved
scallion slices over the stir-fry, and
serve immediately.

stir-fried beef with pearl onions

serves four

1 lb/450 g beef tenderloin

2 tbsp light soy sauce

1 tsp chili oil

1 tbsp tamarind paste

2 tbsp palm sugar or raw
   brown sugar

2 garlic cloves, minced

2 tbsp corn oil

8 oz/225 g pearl onions

2 tbsp chopped fresh cilantro

1 Using a sharp knife, thinly slice the beef.

2 Place the slices of beef in a large, shallow, non-metallic dish.

3 Mix together the soy sauce, chili oil, tamarind paste, palm or raw sugar, and garlic.

4 Spoon the sugar mixture over the beef. Toss well to coat the beef in the mixture, cover with plastic wrap, and let marinate for at least 1 hour.

5 Heat the corn oil in a preheated wok or large skillet.

6 Peel the onions and cut them in half. Add the onions to the wok or skillet and stir-fry for 2–3 minutes, or until just browning.

7 Add the beef and marinade juices to the wok or skillet and cook over high heat for about 5 minutes.

8 Sprinkle with chopped fresh cilantro and serve immediately.

red-hot beef with cashew nuts

serves four

1 lb 2 oz/500 g boneless, lean beef
   sirloin, sliced thinly

1 tsp vegetable oil

1 tsp sesame oil

4 tbsp unsalted cashew nuts

1 scallion, thickly sliced diagonally

cucumber slices, to garnish

MARINADE

1 tbsp sesame seeds

1 garlic clove, chopped

1 tbsp finely chopped
   fresh gingerroot

1 fresh red bird-eye chile, chopped

2 tbsp dark soy sauce

1 tsp Thai red curry paste

freshly cooked rice, to serve

1 Cut the beef into ½-inch-/1-cm-wide strips. Place them in a large, nonmetallic bowl.

2 To make the marinade, dry-fry the sesame seeds in a wok or heavy skillet over medium heat for 2–3 minutes.

3 Place the seeds in a mortar with the garlic, ginger, and chile and grind to a smooth paste with a pestle. Add the soy sauce and curry paste and mix well.

4 Spoon the paste over the beef strips and toss well to coat the meat evenly. Cover and let marinate in the refrigerator for at least 2–3 hours or overnight.

5 Heat a heavy skillet or wok until very hot and brush with vegetable oil. Add the beef strips and cook quickly, turning frequently, until lightly browned. Remove from the heat and spoon into a pile in a warmed serving dish.

6 Heat the sesame oil in a small pan and fry the cashew nuts until golden. Add the sliced scallion and stir-fry for 30 seconds. Sprinkle the mixture onto the beef and serve, garnished with cucumber.

pork balls with mint sauce

serves four

1 lb 2 oz/500 g lean ground pork

¾ cup fine fresh white bread crumbs

½ tsp ground allspice

1 garlic clove, minced

2 tbsp chopped fresh mint

1 egg, beaten

2 tbsp corn oil

1 red bell pepper, seeded and
    thinly sliced

generous 1 cup chicken bouillon

4 pickled walnuts, sliced

salt and pepper

fresh mint sprigs, to garnish

cooked rice or Chinese noodles,
    to serve

1 Mix the ground pork, bread crumbs, allspice, garlic, and half the chopped mint together in a mixing bowl. Season to taste with salt and pepper, then bind together with the beaten egg.

2 Shape the meat mixture into 20 small balls with your hands, damping your hands if it is easier for shaping.

3 Heat the corn oil in a preheated wok or heavy skillet, swirling the oil around until really hot, then add the pork balls, and stir-fry for about 4–5 minutes, or until browned all over.

4 Remove the pork balls from the wok or skillet using a slotted spoon as they are ready and drain thoroughly on paper towels.

5 Pour off all but 1 tablespoon of fat and oil from the wok or skillet, then add the red bell pepper, and stir-fry for 2–3 minutes, or until the slices start to soften, but not color.

6 Add the chicken bouillon and bring to a boil. Season well with salt and pepper and return the pork balls to the wok or skillet, stirring to coat in the sauce. Let simmer for 7–10 minutes, turning the pork balls from time to time.

7 Add the remaining chopped mint and the pickled walnuts and continue to simmer for 2–3 minutes, turning the pork balls regularly to coat them in the sauce.

8 Adjust the seasoning and serve the pork balls with rice or Chinese noodles, and garnished with fresh mint sprigs.

sweet-&-sour pork

serves four

1 lb/450 g pork tenderloin

2 tbsp corn oil

8 oz/225 g zucchini

1 red onion, cut into thin wedges

2 garlic cloves, minced

3 carrots, cut into thin sticks

1 red bell pepper, seeded
    and sliced

3½ oz/100 g baby corn cobs

3½ oz/100 g white
    mushrooms, halved

1¼ cups fresh cubed pineapple

1 cup bean sprouts

⅔ cup pineapple juice

1 tbsp cornstarch

2 tbsp soy sauce

3 tbsp tomato catsup

1 tbsp white wine vinegar

1 tbsp honey

COOK'S TIP

If you prefer a crisper
coating, toss the pork in
a mixture of cornstarch and
egg white and deep-fry in
the wok in step 2.

1 Using a sharp knife, thinly slice the pork into even-size pieces.

2 Heat the corn oil in a large preheated wok. Add the pork to the wok and stir-fry for 10 minutes, or until the pork is completely cooked through and starting to turn crisp at the edges.

3 Meanwhile, cut the zucchini into thin sticks.

4 Add the onion, garlic, carrots, zucchini, bell pepper, corn cobs, and mushrooms to the wok, and cook for an additional 5 minutes.

5 Add the pineapple cubes and bean sprouts to the wok and cook for 2 minutes.

6 Mix the pineapple juice, cornstarch, soy sauce, tomato catsup, white wine vinegar, and honey in a bowl.

7 Pour the sweet-and-sour mixture into the wok and cook over high heat, tossing frequently, until the juices thicken. Transfer the sweet-and-sour pork to serving bowls and serve hot.

pork tenderloin with crunchy satay sauce

serves four

2 small carrots

2 tbsp corn oil

12 oz/350 g pork tenderloin,
    sliced thinly

1 onion, sliced

2 garlic cloves, minced

1 yellow bell pepper, seeded
    and sliced

5½ oz/150 g snow peas

2¾ oz/75 g fine asparagus

chopped salted peanuts, to serve

SATAY SAUCE

6 tbsp crunchy peanut butter

6 tbsp coconut milk

1 tsp chili flakes

1 garlic clove, minced

1 tsp tomato paste

1 Using a sharp knife, slice the carrots into thin sticks.

2 Heat the corn oil in a preheated wok. Add the pork, onion, and garlic and cook for 5 minutes, or until the pork is cooked through.

3 Add the carrots, bell pepper, snow peas, and asparagus to the wok, and cook for 5 minutes.

4 To make the satay sauce, place the peanut butter, coconut milk, chili flakes, garlic, and tomato paste in a small pan and heat gently, stirring, until well combined. Be careful not to let the sauce stick to the bottom of the pan.

5 Transfer the stir-fry to warmed serving plates. Spoon the satay sauce over the stir-fry and sprinkle with chopped peanuts. Serve immediately.

stir-fried pork with pasta & vegetables

serves four

3 tbsp corn oil

12 oz/350 g pork tenderloin, cut
    into thin strips

1 lb/450 g dried taglioni

8 shallots, sliced

2 garlic cloves, chopped finely

1-inch/2.5-cm piece fresh
    gingerroot, grated

1 fresh green chile, chopped finely

1 red bell pepper, seeded and
    thinly sliced

1 green bell pepper, seeded and
    thinly sliced

3 zucchini, sliced thinly

2 tbsp ground almonds

1 tsp ground cinnamon

1 tbsp oyster sauce

1 cup coconut cream

salt and pepper

cook for about 10 minutes, until just
done. Drain the pasta thoroughly, set
aside, and keep warm.

1 Heat the corn oil in a preheated
wok. Season the pork with salt
and pepper to taste, add to the wok,
and stir-fry for 5 minutes.

2 Meanwhile, bring a large pan of
lightly salted water to a boil. Add
the taglioni, bring back to a boil, and

3 Add the shallots, garlic, ginger,
and chile to the wok and stir-fry
for 2 minutes. Add the bell peppers
and zucchini and stir-fry for 1 minute.

4 Finally, add the ground almonds,
ground cinnamon, oyster sauce,
and coconut cream to the wok and
stir-fry for 1 minute.

5 Transfer the taglioni to a warmed
serving dish. Top with the stir-fry
and serve immediately.

five-spice crispy pork with egg-fried rice

serves four

1¼ cups long-grain white rice

2½ cups cold water

12 oz/350 g pork tenderloin

2 tsp Chinese five-spice powder

4 tbsp cornstarch

3 extra large eggs

2 tbsp raw brown sugar

2 tbsp corn oil

1 onion

2 garlic cloves, minced

1 large carrot, diced

1 red bell pepper, seeded and diced

scant 1 cup peas

1 tbsp butter

salt and pepper

1 Rinse the rice in a strainer under cold running water. Place the rice in a large pan, add the cold water and a pinch of salt. Bring to a boil, cover, then reduce the heat, and let simmer for about 9 minutes, or until all of the liquid has been absorbed and the rice is tender.

2 Meanwhile, slice the pork into very thin, even-size pieces, using a sharp knife or meat cleaver. Set the pork strips aside until required.

3 Stir together the Chinese five-spice powder, cornstarch, 1 egg, and the raw brown sugar. Toss the pork in the mixture until coated.

4 Heat the corn oil in a preheated wok or skillet. Add the pork and cook over high heat until the pork is cooked through and crisp. Remove the pork from the wok with a slotted spoon and keep warm until required.

5 Using a sharp knife, cut the onion into dice.

6 Add the onion, garlic, carrot, bell pepper, and peas to the wok and stir-fry for 5 minutes.

7 Return the pork to the wok together with the cooked rice and stir-fry for 5 minutes.

8 Heat the butter in a skillet. Beat the remaining eggs, add to the skillet, and cook until set. Turn out onto a clean board and slice thinly. Toss the strips of egg into the rice mixture and serve immediately.

pork with daikon

4 tbsp vegetable oil

1 lb/450 g pork tenderloin

1 eggplant

8 oz/225 g daikon

2 garlic cloves, minced

3 tbsp light soy sauce

2 tbsp sweet chili sauce

cooked rice or noodles, to serve

COOK'S TIP

Daikon are long white vegetables common in Chinese cooking. Usually grated, they have a milder flavor than red radish. They are generally available in most large food stores.

1 Heat 2 tablespoons of the vegetable oil in a large preheated wok or skillet.

2 Using a sharp knife, thinly slice the pork into even-size pieces.

3 Add the slices of pork to the wok or skillet and stir-fry for about 5 minutes.

4 Using a sharp knife, trim the eggplant and cut into dice. Peel and slice the daikon.

5 Add the remaining vegetable oil to the wok.

6 Add the diced eggplant to the wok or skillet together with the garlic and stir-fry for 5 minutes.

7 Add the daikon to the wok and stir-fry for about 2 minutes.

8 Stir in the soy and chili sauces and cook until heated through.

9 Transfer the pork and daikon to warmed serving bowls and serve immediately with rice or noodles.

twice-cooked pork with bell peppers

serves four

½ oz/15 g dried shiitake mushrooms

1 lb/450 g pork leg steaks

2 tbsp vegetable oil

1 onion, sliced

1 red bell pepper, seeded and diced

1 green bell pepper, seeded
and diced

1 yellow bell pepper, seeded
and diced

4 tbsp oyster sauce

VARIATION

Use open-cap mushrooms,
sliced, instead of shiitake
mushrooms, if you like.

1 Place the mushrooms in a large bowl. Pour over enough boiling water to cover and let stand for 20 minutes.

2 Using a sharp knife, trim any excess fat from the pork steaks, then cut the pork into thin strips.

3 Bring a large pan of water to a boil. Add the pork to the boiling water and cook for 5 minutes.

4 Remove the pork from the pan with a slotted spoon and leave to drain thoroughly.

5 Heat the vegetable oil in a preheated wok. Add the pork to the wok and stir-fry for 5 minutes.

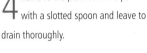

6 Remove the mushrooms from the water and drain thoroughly. Coarsely chop the mushrooms.

7 Add the mushrooms, onion, and bell peppers to the wok and stir-fry for 5 minutes.

8 Stir in the oyster sauce and cook for 2–3 minutes. Transfer to serving bowls and serve immediately.

spicy pork balls

serves four

1 lb/450 g ground pork

2 shallots, chopped finely

2 garlic cloves, minced

1 tsp cumin seeds

½ tsp chili powder

½ cup fresh whole-wheat
  bread crumbs

1 egg, beaten

2 tbsp corn oil

14 oz/400 g canned chopped
  tomatoes, flavored with chili

2 tbsp soy sauce

7 oz/200 g canned water chestnuts,
  drained and rinsed

3 tbsp chopped fresh cilantro

COOK'S TIP

Add a few teaspoons of chili
sauce to a can of chopped
tomatoes, if you can't find the
flavored variety.

1 Place the ground pork in a large mixing bowl. Add the shallots, garlic, cumin seeds, chili powder, bread crumbs, and beaten egg, and mix together well.

2 Form the mixture into balls between the damped palms of your hands.

3 Heat the corn oil in a large preheated wok. Add the pork balls and stir-fry, in batches, over high heat for about 5 minutes, or until sealed on all sides.

4 Add the tomatoes, soy sauce, and water chestnuts and bring to a boil. Return the pork balls to the wok, reduce the heat, and let simmer for 15 minutes.

5 Sprinkle with chopped fresh cilantro and serve hot.

pork with plums

serves four

1 lb/450 g pork tenderloin

1 tbsp cornstarch

2 tbsp light soy sauce

2 tbsp Chinese rice wine

4 tsp light brown sugar

pinch of ground cinnamon

5 tsp vegetable oil

2 garlic cloves, minced

2 scallions, chopped

4 tbsp plum sauce

1 tbsp hoisin sauce

⅔ cup water

dash of chili sauce

TO GARNISH

fried plum fourths

scallions

1 Using a sharp knife, cut the pork tenderloin into thin slices.

2 Mix the cornstarch, soy sauce, rice wine, sugar, and cinnamon together in a small bowl.

3 Place the pork in a shallow dish and pour the cornstarch mixture over it. Toss the meat in the marinade until it is completely coated. Cover and let marinate for at least 30 minutes.

4 Remove the pork from the dish and set aside the marinade.

5 Heat the vegetable oil in a preheated wok or skillet. Add the pork and cook for 3–4 minutes, until a light golden color.

6 Stir in the garlic, scallions, plum sauce, hoisin sauce, water, and chili sauce. Bring the sauce to a boil. Reduce the heat, cover, and let simmer for 8–10 minutes, or until the pork is cooked through and tender.

7 Stir in the reserved marinade and cook, stirring, for about 5 minutes.

8 Transfer the pork stir-fry to a warmed serving dish and garnish with fried plum fourths and scallions. Serve immediately.

garlic lamb with soy sauce

serves four

1 lb/450 g lamb loin

2 garlic cloves

2 tbsp peanut oil

3 tbsp dry sherry or Chinese rice wine

3 tbsp dark soy sauce

1 tsp cornstarch

2 tbsp water

2 tbsp butter

1 Using a sharp knife, make small slits in the flesh of the lamb.

2 Carefully peel the garlic cloves and cut them into slices, using a sharp knife.

3 Push the slices of garlic into the slits in the lamb. Place the lamb in a shallow dish.

4 In a small bowl, mix 1 tablespoon each of the peanut oil, dry sherry or rice wine, and dark soy sauce. Drizzle this mixture over the lamb, cover with plastic wrap, and let marinate in the refrigerator for at least 1 hour, preferably overnight.

5 Drain the lamb and, using a sharp knife or meat cleaver, thinly slice the meat. Set aside the marinade.

6 Heat the remaining oil in a preheated wok or large skillet. Add the marinated lamb and stir-fry for 5 minutes.

7 Add the marinade juices, the remaining sherry and soy sauce to the wok or skillet and let the juices bubble for 5 minutes.

8 Blend the cornstarch to a smooth paste with the water. Add the cornstarch mixture to the wok or skillet and cook, stirring occasionally, until the juices start to thicken.

9 Cut the butter into small pieces. Add the butter to the wok or skillet and stir until the butter melts. Transfer the lamb to serving dishes and serve immediately.

thai-style lamb with lime leaves

serves four

2 fresh red chiles

2 tbsp peanut oil

2 garlic, cloves minced

4 shallots, chopped

2 lemongrass stalks, sliced

6 kaffir lime leaves

1 tbsp tamarind paste

2 tbsp palm sugar

1 lb/450 g lean lamb (leg or loin)

2½ cups coconut milk

6 oz/175 g cherry tomatoes, halved

1 tbsp chopped fresh cilantro

freshly cooked fragrant rice,
    to serve

COOK'S TIP

When buying fresh cilantro,
look for bright green, unwilted
leaves. To store it, wash and
dry the leaves, leaving them
on the stem. Wrap the leaves
in damp paper towels and
keep them in a plastic bag
in the refrigerator.

1 Using a sharp knife, seed and very finely chop the red chiles.

2 Heat the peanut oil in a large preheated wok or skillet.

3 Add the minced garlic, shallots, lemongrass, lime leaves, tamarind paste, palm sugar, and chiles and stir-fry for about 2 minutes.

4 Using a sharp knife, cut the lamb into thin strips or cubes. Add the lamb to the wok or skillet and stir-fry for about 5 minutes, tossing well so that the lamb is evenly coated in the spice mixture.

5 Pour the coconut milk into the wok or skillet and bring to a boil. Reduce the heat and let simmer gently for 20 minutes.

6 Add the tomatoes and cilantro and let simmer for 5 minutes. Transfer to serving plates and serve with freshly cooked fragrant rice.

lamb with black bean sauce & bell peppers

serves four

1 lb/450 g boneless leg of lamb

1 egg white, beaten lightly

4 tbsp cornstarch

1 tsp Chinese five-spice powder

3 tbsp corn oil

1 red onion

1 red bell pepper, seeded and sliced

1 green bell pepper, seeded
  and sliced

1 yellow or orange bell pepper,
  seeded and sliced

5 tbsp black bean sauce

cooked rice or noodles, to serve

1 Using a sharp knife, slice the lamb into very thin strips.

2 Mix the egg white, cornstarch, and Chinese five-spice powder. Toss the lamb strips in the mixture until evenly coated.

3 Heat the corn oil in a preheated wok and stir-fry the lamb over high heat for 5 minutes, or until it crispens around the edges.

4 Slice the red onion. Add the onion and bell pepper slices to the wok and stir-fry for 5–6 minutes, or until the vegetables just start to soften.

5 Stir the black bean sauce into the mixture and heat through.

6 Transfer the lamb and sauce to warmed individual serving plates and serve immediately with freshly cooked rice or noodles.

scallions & lamb stir-fry with oyster sauce

serves four

1 lb/450 g lamb leg steaks

1 tsp ground Szechuan peppercorns

1 tbsp peanut oil

2 garlic cloves, minced

8 scallions, sliced

2 tbsp dark soy sauce

6 oz/175 g Napa cabbage

6 tbsp oyster sauce

shrimp crackers, to serve (optional)

COOK'S TIP

Oyster sauce is made from oysters, which are cooked in brine and soy sauce. Sold in bottles, it will keep in the refrigerator for months.

1 Using a sharp knife, remove any excess fat from the lamb. Slice the lamb thinly.

2 Sprinkle the ground Szechuan peppercorns over the meat and toss together until well mixed.

3 Heat the peanut oil in a preheated wok or large skillet.

4 Add the slices of lamb to the wok or skillet and cook for about 5 minutes.

5 Crush the garlic cloves with a pestle and mortar and slice the scallions. Add the garlic and scallions to the wok, together with the dark soy sauce, and stir-fry for 2 minutes.

6 Coarsely shred the Napa cabbage leaves and add them to the wok or skillet together with the oyster sauce. Stir-fry for an additional 2 minutes, or until the cabbage has wilted and the juices are bubbling.

7 Transfer the lamb stir-fry to warmed individual serving bowls and serve immediately with shrimp crackers (if using).

lamb with satay sauce

serves four

1 lb/450 g lamb loin

1 tbsp mild curry paste

⅔ cup coconut milk

2 garlic cloves, minced

½ tsp chili powder

½ tsp cumin

SATAY SAUCE

1 tbsp corn oil

1 onion, diced

6 tbsp crunchy peanut butter

1 tsp tomato paste

1 tsp fresh lime juice

generous ⅓ cup water

COOK'S TIP

Soak the wooden skewers
in cold water for 30 minutes
before broiling to prevent
them from burning.

---

1 Using a sharp knife, thinly slice the lamb and place in a large dish.

2 Mix the curry paste, coconut milk, garlic, chili powder, and cumin in a bowl. Pour over the lamb, toss well, cover with plastic wrap, and let marinate for 30 minutes.

3 To make the satay sauce, heat the oil in a preheated wok and stir-fry the onion for 5 minutes, then reduce the heat, and cook for 5 minutes.

4 Stir in the peanut butter, tomato paste, lime juice, and water.

5 Thread the lamb onto wooden skewers. Set aside the marinade.

6 Broil the lamb skewers for 6–8 minutes, turning once.

7 Add the reserved marinade to the wok, bring to a boil, and cook for 5 minutes. Serve the lamb skewers with the satay sauce.

stir-fried lamb with orange

serves four

1 lb/450 g ground lamb

2 garlic cloves, minced

1 tsp cumin seeds

1 tsp ground coriander

1 red onion, sliced

finely grated peel and juice of
   1 orange

2 tbsp light soy sauce

1 orange, peeled and segmented

salt and pepper

snipped fresh chives, to garnish

1 Heat a wok or large heavy skillet, without adding any oil.

2 Add the ground lamb to the wok or skillet. Dry-fry the ground lamb for 5 minutes, or until the meat is evenly browned. Drain away any excess fat.

3 Add the garlic, cumin seeds, coriander, and red onion to the wok or skillet and stir-fry for 5 minutes.

4 Stir in the finely grated orange peel and juice and the soy sauce, mixing until thoroughly blended.

Cover, reduce the heat, and let simmer, stirring occasionally, for 15 minutes.

5 Remove the lid, increase the heat and add the orange segments. Stir to mix.

6 Season to taste with salt and pepper and heat through for an additional 2–3 minutes.

7 Transfer the lamb stir-fry to warmed individual serving plates and garnish with snipped fresh chives. Serve immediately.

lamb's liver with bell peppers & sherry

serves four

1 lb/450 g lamb's liver

3 tbsp cornstarch

2 tbsp peanut oil

1 onion, sliced

2 garlic cloves, minced

2 green bell peppers, seeded
   and sliced

2 tbsp tomato paste

3 tbsp dry sherry

2 tbsp dark soy sauce

1 Using a sharp knife, trim any excess fat from the lamb's liver. Slice the lamb's liver into thin strips.

2 Place 2 tablespoons of the cornstarch in a large bowl.

3 Add the strips of lamb's liver to the cornstarch and toss well until coated evenly all over.

4 Heat the peanut oil in a large preheated wok.

5 Add the lamb's liver, onion, garlic, and green bell pepper to the wok and stir-fry for 6–7 minutes, or until the lamb's liver is just cooked through and the vegetables are tender.

6 Mix the tomato paste, dry sherry, the remaining cornstarch, and the soy sauce in a bowl. Stir the mixture into the wok and cook, stirring constantly, for an additional 2 minutes, or until the juices have thickened. Transfer to warmed individual serving bowls and serve immediately.

sweet-&-sour venison stir-fry

serves four

bunch of scallions

1 red bell pepper

1½ cups snow peas

1 cup baby corn cobs

12 oz/350 g lean venison steak

1 tbsp vegetable oil

1 garlic clove, minced

1-inch/2.5-cm piece fresh
    gingerroot, chopped finely

3 tbsp light soy sauce, plus extra
    for serving

1 tbsp white wine vinegar

2 tbsp dry sherry

2 tsp honey

8 oz/225 g canned pineapple pieces
    in natural juice, drained

½ cup bean sprouts

cooked rice, to serve

1 Cut the scallions into 1-inch/
2.5-cm pieces. Halve and seed
the red bell pepper and cut it into
1-inch/2.5-cm pieces. Trim the snow
peas and baby corn cobs.

2 Trim any fat from the meat and
cut it into thin strips. Heat the
vegetable oil in a preheated wok or
large skillet until hot and stir-fry the
meat, garlic, and ginger for 5 minutes.

3 Add the scallions, red bell pepper,
snow peas, and baby corn cobs,
then stir in the soy sauce, white wine
vinegar, sherry, and honey. Stir-fry for
an additional 5 minutes.

4 Carefully stir in the pineapple
pieces and bean sprouts and cook
for 1–2 minutes to heat through. Serve
with freshly cooked rice and extra soy
sauce for dipping.

VARIATION

For a nutritious meal-in-one,
cook 8 oz/225 g egg noodles in
boiling water for 3–4 minutes.
Drain and add to the wok in
step 4, with the pineapple and
bean sprouts. Add an extra
2 tablespoons soy sauce with the
pineapple and bean sprouts.

Fish & Shellfish

Throughout the Far Eastern countries, fish and

shellfish play a major role in the diet of the

inhabitants; this is because these foods are

both plentiful and very healthy. They are also very versatile: there are many

different ways of cooking fish and shellfish in a wok—they may be steamed,

deep-fried, or cooked with a range of delicious spices and sauces.

Japan is famed for its sushimi, or raw fish, but this is just one of the wide

range of fish dishes served. Fish and shellfish are offered at every meal in

Japan, many of them cooked in a wok.

When buying fish and shellfish for the recipes in this chapter, freshness is

imperative to flavor, so be sure to buy and use the fish that you have chosen

as soon as possible, preferably on the same day.

tuna & vegetable stir-fry

serves four

3 small carrots

1 onion

1½ cups baby corn cobs

2 tbsp corn oil

2¼ cups snow peas

1 lb/450 g fresh tuna

2 tbsp Thai fish sauce

1 tbsp palm sugar

finely grated peel and juice of

    1 orange

2 tbsp sherry

1 tsp cornstarch

cooked rice or noodles, to serve

VARIATION

Try using swordfish steaks
instead of the tuna. Swordfish
steaks are now widely
available and are similar
in texture to tuna.

---

1 Using a sharp knife, cut the carrots into thin sticks, slice the onion, and halve the baby corn cobs.

2 Heat the corn oil in a large preheated wok or skillet.

3 Add the onion, carrots, snow peas, and baby corn cobs to the wok or skillet and stir-fry over medium heat for 5 minutes.

4 Using a sharp knife, thinly slice the fresh tuna. (This is easier if it has been chilled in the freezer.)

5 Add the tuna slices to the wok or skillet and stir-fry for about 2–3 minutes, or until the tuna turns opaque.

6 Mix the fish sauce, palm sugar, orange peel and juice, sherry, and cornstarch together.

7 Pour the mixture over the tuna and vegetables and cook for 2 minutes, or until the juices thicken. Serve the stir-fry with rice or noodles.

stir-fried ginger monkfish

serves four

1 lb/450 g monkfish tail

1 tbsp grated fresh gingerroot

2 tbsp sweet chili sauce

1 tbsp corn oil

3½ oz/100 g fine asparagus

3 scallions, sliced

1 tsp sesame oil

1 Carefully remove all the gray membrane covering the monkfish. Using a sharp knife, cut along the monkfish tail on either side of the central bone. Remove and discard the bone. Slice the flesh into thin, flat rounds. Set aside.

2 Mix the grated gingerroot and sweet chili sauce in a small bowl, stirring until they are thoroughly blended. Brush the ginger and chili sauce mixture over the monkfish pieces, using a pastry brush.

3 Heat the corn oil in a large preheated wok or heavy skillet.

4 Add the monkfish pieces, asparagus, and scallions to the wok or skillet and stir-fry over medium heat for about 5 minutes, or until the fish is opaque and flakes easily. Stir the mixture gently so the fish pieces do not break up.

5 Remove the wok or skillet from the heat, drizzle the sesame oil over the stir-fry, and toss gently to combine.

6 Transfer the stir-fried ginger monkfish to warmed serving plates and serve immediately.

monkfish & okra balti

serves four

1 lb 10 oz/750 g monkfish fillet, cut
   into 1¼-inch/3-cm cubes

9 oz/250 g okra

2 tbsp corn oil

1 onion, sliced

1 garlic clove, minced

1-inch/2.5-cm piece fresh
   gingerroot, sliced

⅔ cup coconut milk or fish bouillon

2 tsp garam masala

MARINADE

3 tbsp lemon juice

grated peel of 1 lemon

¼ tsp aniseed

½ tsp salt

½ tsp pepper

TO GARNISH

4 lime wedges

fresh cilantro sprigs

1 To make the marinade, mix all the ingredients in a bowl. Stir the monkfish into the bowl, cover and let marinate for 1 hour.

2 Bring a pan of water to a boil, add the okra, and let simmer for 4–5 minutes. Drain well and cut into ½-inch/1-cm slices.

3 Heat the corn oil in a wok or skillet, add the onion, and stir-fry until golden brown. Add the garlic and ginger and stir-fry for 1 minute. Add the fish with the marinade and stir-fry for an additional 2 minutes.

4 Stir in the okra, coconut milk or bouillon, and the garam masala and let simmer for 10 minutes. Serve garnished with lime wedges and fresh cilantro sprigs.

119

fried fish with coconut & basil

serves four

2 tbsp vegetable oil

1 lb/450 g cod fillet, skinned

3 tbsp seasoned flour

1 garlic clove, minced

2 tbsp red curry paste

1 tbsp Thai fish sauce

1¼ cups coconut milk

6 oz/175 g cherry tomatoes, halved

20 fresh basil leaves

freshly cooked fragrant rice, to serve

COOK'S TIP

Take care not to overcook the dish once the tomatoes are added, otherwise they will break down and the skins will come away.

1 Heat the vegetable oil in a large preheated wok.

2 Using a sharp knife, cut the fish into large cubes, removing any bones with a pair of clean tweezers.

3 Place the seasoned flour in a bowl. Add the cubes of fish and mix until well coated.

4 Add the coated fish to the wok and cook over high heat for 3–4 minutes, or until the fish just starts to brown at the edges.

5 In a small bowl, mix the garlic, curry paste, fish sauce, and coconut milk. Pour the mixture over the fish and bring to a boil.

6 Add the tomatoes and let simmer for 5 minutes.

7 Coarsely chop or tear the fresh basil leaves. Add the basil to the wok and stir to combine, taking care not to break up the cubes of fish.

8 Transfer to serving plates and serve hot with freshly cooked fragrant rice.

stir-fried cod with mango

serves four

2 carrots

2 tbsp vegetable oil

1 red onion, sliced

1 red bell pepper, seeded and sliced

1 green bell pepper, seeded
   and sliced

1 lb/450 g cod fillet, skinned

1 ripe mango

1 tsp cornstarch

1 tbsp light soy sauce

generous ⅓ cup tropical fruit juice

1 tbsp lime juice

1 tbsp chopped fresh cilantro,
   to garnish

1 Using a sharp knife, slice the carrots into thin sticks.

2 Heat the oil in a preheated wok and stir-fry the onion, carrots, and bell peppers for 5 minutes.

3 Using a sharp knife, cut the cod into small cubes. Peel the mango, then carefully remove the flesh from the center pit. Cut the flesh into thin slices.

4 Add the cod and mango to the wok and stir-fry for 4–5 minutes, or until the fish is cooked through. Be careful not to break up the fish.

5 Mix the cornstarch, soy sauce, fruit juice, and lime juice. Pour the mixture into the wok and stir until the mixture bubbles and the juices thicken. Sprinkle with cilantro and serve immediately.

braised fish fillets

serves four

3–4 small dried shiitake mushrooms

10½–12 oz/300–350 g fish fillets

1 tsp salt

½ egg white, beaten lightly

1 tsp cornstarch

2½ cups vegetable oil

1 tsp finely chopped
    fresh gingerroot

2 scallions, chopped finely

1 garlic clove, chopped finely

½ small green bell pepper, seeded
    and cut into small cubes

½ small carrot, sliced thinly

½ cup canned bamboo shoots,
    rinsed and sliced

½ tsp sugar

1 tbsp light soy sauce

1 tsp Chinese rice wine or dry sherry

1 tbsp chili bean sauce

2–3 tbsp vegetable bouillon or water

few drops of sesame oil

1 Soak the dried mushrooms in a bowl of warm water for 30 minutes. Drain thoroughly on paper towels. Set aside the soaking water for bouillon or soup. Squeeze the mushrooms to extract all of the moisture, cut off and discard any hard stems, and slice thinly.

2 Cut the fish into bite-size pieces, then place in a shallow dish and mix with a pinch of salt, the egg white, and cornstarch, turning the fish to coat on all sides.

3 Heat the oil in a preheated wok. Add the fish pieces to the wok and deep-fry for about 1 minute. Remove the fish pieces with a slotted spoon and drain on paper towels.

4 Pour off the excess oil, leaving about 1 tablespoon in the wok. Add the ginger, scallions, and garlic to flavor the oil for a few seconds, then add the bell pepper, carrot, and bamboo shoots, and stir-fry for about 1 minute.

5 Add the sugar, soy sauce, rice wine, chili bean sauce, bouillon or water, and the remaining salt, and bring to a boil. Add the fish pieces, stirring to coat with the sauce, and braise for 1 minute. Sprinkle with sesame oil and serve immediately.

coconut shrimp

serves four

½ cup dry unsweetened coconut

½ cup fresh white bread crumbs

1 tsp Chinese five-spice powder

½ tsp salt

finely grated peel of 1 lime

1 egg white

1 lb/450 g raw fan-tail shrimp

corn oil

lemon wedges, to garnish

soy or chili sauce, to serve

COOK'S TIP

If the shrimp are frozen, thaw them thoroughly before cooking. Raw shrimp are best for this dish, but if you cannot obtain them, buy unshelled cooked shrimp and shell them yourself.

1 Mix the dry unsweetened coconut, white bread crumbs, Chinese five-spice powder, salt, and lime peel in a bowl.

2 Lightly whisk the egg white in a separate bowl.

3 Rinse the shrimp under cold running water, and pat dry with paper towels.

4 Dip the shrimp into the egg white, then into the coconut and bread crumb mixture, so that they are evenly coated.

5 Heat about 2 inches/5 cm of corn oil in a large preheated wok.

6 Add the shrimp to the wok and cook for about 5 minutes, or until golden and crisp.

7 Remove the shrimp with a slotted spoon and drain on paper towels.

8 Transfer the coconut shrimp to warmed serving dishes and garnish with lemon wedges. Serve immediately with soy or chili sauce.

shrimp omelet

serves four

2 tbsp corn oil

4 scallions

12 oz/350 g cooked shelled shrimp

1 cup bean sprouts

1 tsp cornstarch

1 tbsp light soy sauce

6 eggs

3 tbsp cold water

1 Heat the corn oil in a large preheated wok or skillet.

2 Using a sharp knife, trim the scallions and cut into slices.

3 Add the shrimp, scallions, and bean sprouts to the wok or skillet and stir-fry for 2 minutes.

4 In a small bowl, mix the cornstarch and soy sauce until all the ingredients are well mixed.

5 In a separate bowl, beat the eggs with the water, using a fork, then blend with the cornstarch and soy mixture.

6 Add the egg mixture to the wok or skillet and cook for 5–6 minutes, or until the mixture sets.

7 Transfer the omelet to a warmed serving plate and cut into fourths to serve.

shrimp with spicy tomatoes

serves four

2 tbsp corn oil

1 onion

2 garlic cloves, minced

1 tsp cumin seeds

1 tbsp brown sugar

14 oz/400 g canned
    chopped tomatoes

1 tbsp sun-dried tomato paste

1 tbsp chopped fresh basil

1 lb/450 g raw jumbo shrimp, shelled

salt and pepper

COOK'S TIP

Cut along the back of each shrimp with a sharp knife and remove the dark vein with the point of the knife.

1 Heat the corn oil in a large preheated wok or heavy skillet.

2 Using a sharp knife, finely chop the onion.

3 Add the onion and garlic to the wok and stir-fry for 2–3 minutes, or until softened.

4 Stir in the cumin seeds and stir-fry for 1 minute.

5 Add the sugar, chopped tomatoes, and sun-dried tomato paste to the wok. Bring the mixture to a boil, then reduce the heat, and let simmer gently for 10 minutes.

6 Add the basil, shrimp, and salt and pepper to taste to the mixture in the wok. Increase the heat and cook for an additional 2–3 minutes, or until the shrimp are completely cooked through. Serve immediately.

spicy thai seafood stew

serves four

7 oz/200 g prepared squid

1 lb 2 oz/500 g firm white fish fillet, preferably monkfish or halibut

1 tbsp corn oil

4 shallots, chopped finely

2 garlic cloves, chopped finely

2 tbsp Thai green curry paste

2 small lemongrass stalks, chopped finely

1 tsp shrimp paste

2¼ cups coconut milk

7 oz/200 g raw jumbo shrimp, shelled

12 live clams, scrubbed

8 fresh basil leaves, shredded finely, plus extra to garnish

cooked rice, to serve

COOK'S TIP

If you like, fresh mussels in shells can be used instead of clams—add them in step 4 and follow the recipe.

1 Cut the squid body cavities into thick rings and cut the fish fillet into bite-size chunks.

2 Heat the corn oil in a preheated wok or large skillet and stir-fry the shallots, garlic, and curry paste over medium heat for 1–2 minutes. Add the lemongrass and shrimp paste, stir in the coconut milk, and bring to a boil.

3 Reduce the heat to low. When the liquid is simmering gently, add the white fish chunks, squid rings, and jumbo shrimp to the wok or skillet. Stir, then let simmer for 2 minutes.

4 Add the clams and simmer for an additional 1 minute, until the clams have opened. Discard any clams that do not open.

5 Sprinkle the shredded basil leaves over the seafood stew and serve immediately, garnished with whole basil leaves and spooned over cooked rice.

vegetables with shrimp & egg

serves four

8 oz/225 g zucchini

3 tbsp vegetable oil

2 eggs

2 tbsp water

3 carrots, grated

1 onion, sliced

1½ cups bean sprouts

8 oz/225 g cooked shelled shrimp

2 tbsp soy sauce

pinch of Chinese five-spice powder

¼ cup peanuts, chopped

2 tbsp chopped fresh cilantro

1 Finely grate the zucchini by hand or in a food processor.

2 Heat 1 tablespoon of the vegetable oil in a large preheated wok.

3 Beat the eggs with the water, pour the mixture into the wok, and cook for 2–3 minutes, or until the omelet sets.

4 Remove the omelet from the wok and transfer to a board. Fold the omelet, cut it into thin strips, and set aside until required.

5 Add the remaining oil to the wok. Add the carrots, onion, and zucchini and stir-fry for 5 minutes.

6 Add the bean sprouts and shrimp to the wok and stir-fry for an additional 2 minutes, or until the shrimp are heated through.

7 Add the soy sauce, Chinese five-spice powder, and peanuts to the wok, together with the strips of omelet and heat through. Transfer to warmed serving bowls, garnish with chopped fresh cilantro, and serve.

shrimp with crisp ginger

serves four

2-inch/5-cm piece fresh gingerroot

peanut oil, for cooking

1 onion, diced

3 small carrots, diced

1 cup frozen peas

1 cup bean sprouts

1 lb/450 g raw jumbo
    shrimp, shelled

1 tsp Chinese five-spice powder

1 tbsp tomato paste

1 tbsp light soy sauce

1 Using a sharp knife, peel the ginger, then slice it into very thin sticks.

2 Heat about 1 inch/2.5 cm of oil in a large preheated wok. Add the ginger and cook for 1 minute, or until the ginger is crisp. Remove the ginger with a slotted spoon and drain on paper towels.

3 Drain all of the oil from the wok except for about 2 tablespoons. Add the onion and carrots to the wok and stir-fry for 5 minutes. Add the peas and bean sprouts and stir-fry for 2 minutes.

4 Rinse the shrimp under cold running water and pat dry with paper towels.

5 Mix the Chinese five-spice, tomato paste, and soy sauce. Brush the mixture over the shrimp.

6 Add the shrimp to the wok and stir-fry for an additional 2 minutes, or until the shrimp are completely cooked through. Transfer the shrimp mixture to a warmed serving bowl, top with the reserved crisp ginger, and serve.

131

stir-fried crab claws with chili

serves four

1 lb 9 oz/700 g crab claws

1 tbsp corn oil

2 garlic cloves, minced

1 tbsp grated fresh gingerroot

3 fresh red chiles, seeded and
    finely chopped

2 tbsp sweet chili sauce

3 tbsp tomato catsup

1¼ cups cooled fish bouillon

1 tbsp cornstarch

salt and pepper

1 tbsp snipped fresh chives

COOK'S TIP

If crab claws are not easily
available, use a whole crab, cut
into 8 pieces, instead.

1 Gently crack the crab claws with
a nutcracker. This process will
allow the flavors of the chile, garlic,
and ginger to penetrate the crab meat.

2 Heat the corn oil in a large
preheated wok.

3 Add the crab claws to the wok
and stir-fry for about 5 minutes.

4 Add the garlic, ginger, and
chiles to the wok and stir-fry for
1 minute, tossing the crab claws to
coat all over.

5 Mix the sweet chili sauce, tomato
catsup, fish bouillon, and
cornstarch in a small bowl. Add this
mixture to the wok and cook, stirring
occasionally, until the sauce starts to
thicken and reduce slightly.

6 Season the mixture in the wok
with salt and pepper to taste.

7 Transfer the crab claws and chili
sauce to warmed serving dishes,
garnish with snipped fresh chives and
serve immediately.

rice with crab & mussels

serves four

1½ cups long-grain rice

6 oz/175 g white crab meat, fresh,
 canned or frozen (thawed
 if frozen)

2 tbsp corn oil

1-inch/2.5-cm piece fresh
 gingerroot, grated

4 scallions, thinly sliced diagonally

1⅓ cups snow peas, cut into
 2–3 pieces

½ tsp ground turmeric

1 tsp ground cumin

2 x 7 oz/200 g jars mussels, well
 drained, or 12 oz/350 g frozen
 mussels, thawed

15 oz/425 g canned bean sprouts,
 well drained

salt and pepper

2 Extract the crab meat, if you are using fresh crab. Break the meat up into flakes.

3 Heat the corn oil in a preheated wok and stir-fry the ginger and scallions for 1–2 minutes. Add the snow peas and continue to cook for an additional 1 minute. Sprinkle the turmeric, cumin, and seasoning over the vegetables and mix well.

4 Add the crab meat and mussels and stir-fry for 1 minute. Stir in the cooked rice and bean sprouts and stir-fry for 2 minutes, or until hot and well mixed.

5 Adjust the seasoning to taste and serve immediately.

1 Cook the rice in a large pan of lightly salted, boiling water for 12–15 minutes. Drain, rinse with freshly boiled water, and drain well again. Set aside.

curried crab

serves four

2 tbsp mustard oil

1 tbsp ghee

1 onion, chopped finely

2-inch/5-cm piece fresh
gingerroot, grated

2 garlic cloves, peeled but
left whole

1 tsp ground turmeric

1 tsp salt

1 tsp chili powder

2 fresh green chiles, chopped

1 tsp paprika

½ cup brown crab meat

1½ cups white crab meat

1 cup plain yogurt

1 tsp garam masala

fresh cilantro, to garnish

cooked basmati rice, to serve

1 Heat the mustard oil in a large preheated wok or heavy skillet.

2 When it starts to smoke, add the ghee and onion. Stir-fry for 3 minutes over medium heat until the onion is soft.

3 Stir in the grated ginger and whole garlic cloves.

4 Stir in the turmeric, salt, chili powder, chiles, and paprika to the wok or skillet. Mix thoroughly.

5 Increase the heat and add the crab meat and yogurt. Let simmer, stirring occasionally, for 10 minutes, until the sauce is thickened slightly.

6 Sprinkle in garam masala to taste and stir well to mix.

7 Serve hot, over plain basmati rice, garnished with the fresh cilantro either chopped or in sprigs.

crab fried rice

⅔ cup long-grain rice

2 tbsp peanut oil

4½ oz/125 g canned white crab
   meat, drained

1 leek, sliced

1½ cups bean sprouts

2 eggs, beaten

1 tbsp light soy sauce

2 tsp lime juice

1 tsp sesame oil

salt

sliced lime, to garnish

VARIATION

Cooked lobster may be used
instead of the crab for a really
special dish.

---

1 Cook the rice in a pan of boiling salted water for 15 minutes. Drain well, rinse under cold running water and drain again thoroughly.

2 Heat the peanut oil in a preheated wok or heavy skillet until it is really hot.

3 Add the crab meat, leek, and bean sprouts to the wok or skillet and stir-fry for 2–3 minutes. Remove the mixture with a slotted spoon and set aside until required.

4 Add the eggs to the wok and cook, stirring occasionally, for 2–3 minutes, until they start to set.

5 Stir the rice and crab meat mixture into the eggs in the wok.

6 Add the soy sauce and lime juice to the mixture in the wok. Cook for 1 minute, stirring until mixed. Sprinkle with the sesame oil and toss lightly to mix.

7 Transfer the crab fried rice to a serving dish, garnish with the sliced lime, and serve immediately.

baked crab with ginger

serves four

1 large or 2 medium crabs,
   weighing about 1 lb 10 oz/
   750 g in total

2 tbsp Chinese rice wine or
   dry sherry

1 egg, beaten lightly

1 tbsp cornstarch

3–4 tbsp vegetable oil

1 tbsp finely chopped fresh
   gingerroot

3–4 scallions, cut into short lengths

2 tbsp light soy sauce

1 tsp sugar

about 5 tbsp fish bouillon or water

½ tsp sesame oil

fresh cilantro leaves, to garnish

3 Mix the wine or sherry, egg, and cornstarch. Pour the mixture over the crab meat and let marinate for 10–15 minutes.

1 Cut the crab in half from the underbelly. Break off the claws and crack them with the back of a cleaver or a large kitchen knife.

2 Discard the legs and crack the shell, breaking it into several pieces. Discard the feathery gills from both sides of the body and the stomach sac. Place the crab meat in a bowl.

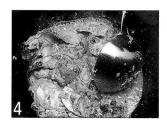

4 Heat the vegetable oil in a preheated wok. Stir-fry the crab meat with the chopped ginger and scallions for 2–3 minutes.

5 Add the soy sauce, sugar, and bouillon or water, blend well, and bring to a boil. Cover and cook for 3–4 minutes, then remove the lid, sprinkle with sesame oil, and serve, garnished with cilantro leaves.

napa cabbage with mushrooms & crab

serves four

8 oz/225 g shiitake mushrooms

2 tbsp vegetable oil

2 garlic cloves, minced

6 scallions, sliced

1 head Napa cabbage, shredded

1 tbsp mild curry paste

6 tbsp coconut milk

7 oz/200 g canned white crab
    meat, drained

1 tsp chili flakes

1 Using a sharp knife, cut the mushrooms into slices.

2 Heat the vegetable oil in a large preheated wok or heavy skillet.

3 Add the mushrooms and garlic to the wok or skillet and stir-fry for 3 minutes, or until the mushrooms have softened.

4 Add the scallions and shredded Napa cabbage to the wok and cook until the leaves have wilted.

5 Mix the mild curry paste and coconut milk in a small bowl.

6 Add the curry paste and coconut milk mixture to the wok, together with the crab meat and chili flakes. Mix together until well combined.

7 Heat the mixture until the juices start to bubble.

8 Transfer the crab and vegetable stir-fry to warmed serving bowls and serve immediately.

mussels in black bean sauce with spinach

serves four

12 oz/350 g leeks

12 oz/350 g cooked, shelled
   green-lipped mussels

1 tsp cumin seeds

2 tbsp vegetable oil

2 garlic cloves, minced

1 red bell pepper, seeded and sliced

1¾ oz/50 g canned bamboo shoots,
   drained and rinsed

6 oz/175 g baby spinach leaves

5¾ oz/160 g jar black bean sauce

COOK'S TIP

If fresh green-lipped mussels are
not available, they can be
bought shelled in cans and jars
from most large food stores.

1 Using a sharp knife, trim the leeks and shred them.

2 Place the cooked green-lipped mussels in a large bowl, sprinkle with the cumin seeds, and toss well to coat all over. Set aside until required.

3 Heat the vegetable oil in a preheated wok, swirling the oil around the bottom of the wok until it is really hot.

4 Add the shredded leeks, garlic, and sliced red bell pepper to the wok and stir-fry for 5 minutes, or until the vegetables are tender.

5 Add the bamboo shoots, baby spinach leaves, and cooked green-lipped mussels to the wok and stir-fry for about 2 minutes.

6 Pour in the black bean sauce, toss well to coat all the ingredients in the sauce, and let simmer for a few seconds, stirring occasionally.

7 Transfer the stir-fry to warmed serving bowls and serve.

scallop crêpes

serves four

3½ oz/100 g fine green beans

1 fresh red chile

1 lb/450 g scallops, without roe

1 egg

3 scallions, sliced

generous ⅓ cup rice flour

1 tbsp Thai fish sauce

oil

salt

sweet chili dip, to serve

1 Using a sharp knife, trim the green beans and slice them very thinly.

2 Seed and very finely chop the red chile.

3 Bring a small pan of lightly salted water to a boil. Add the green beans to the pan and cook for 3–4 minutes, or until just softened.

4 Coarsely chop the scallops and place them in a large bowl. Add the cooked beans to the scallops.

5 Mix the egg, scallions, rice flour, fish sauce, and chile until thoroughly mixed. Add to the scallops and mix well.

6 Heat about 1 inch/2.5 cm of oil in a large preheated wok. Add a ladleful of the mixture to the wok and cook for 5 minutes, until golden and set.

7 Remove the crêpe from the wok and drain on paper towels. Keep warm while cooking the remaining crêpe mixture. Serve the crêpes hot with a sweet chili dip.

seared scallops with butter sauce

serves four

1 lb/450 g fresh scallops, without
   roe, or the same amount of
   frozen scallops, thawed

6 scallions

2 tbsp vegetable oil

1 fresh green chile, seeded
   and sliced

3 tbsp sweet soy sauce

2 tbsp butter, diced

COOK'S TIP

If you buy scallops on the shell,
slide a knife underneath the
membrane to loosen it and cut
off the tough muscle that holds
the scallop to the shell. Discard
the black stomach sac and
intestinal vein.

1 Rinse the scallops thoroughly under cold running water, drain, and pat dry with paper towels.

2 Carefully slice each scallop in half horizontally.

3 Using a sharp knife, trim and slice the scallions.

4 Heat the vegetable oil in a large preheated wok or heavy skillet, swirling the oil around the bottom of the wok or skillet until it is really hot.

5 Add the sliced green chile, scallions, and scallops to the wok or skillet, and stir-fry over high heat for 4–5 minutes, or until the scallops are just cooked through. If using frozen scallops, be sure not to overcook them as they will easily disintegrate.

6 Add the soy sauce and butter to the scallop stir-fry and heat through until the butter melts.

7 Transfer to warmed serving bowls and serve hot.

balti scallops

serves four

1 lb 10 oz/750 g shelled scallops

2 tbsp corn oil

2 onions, chopped

3 tomatoes, cut into fourths

2 fresh green chiles, sliced

4 lime wedges, to garnish

MARINADE

3 tbsp chopped fresh cilantro

1-inch/2.5-cm piece fresh
    gingerroot, grated

1 tsp ground coriander

3 tbsp lemon juice

grated peel of 1 lemon

¼ tsp pepper

½ tsp salt

½ tsp ground cumin

1 garlic clove, minced

COOK'S TIP

It is best to buy the scallops
fresh in the shell with the roe—
you will need 1.5 kg/3 lb 5 oz.
A fishmonger will clean them
and remove the shell for you.

---

1 To make the marinade, mix all the ingredients in a bowl.

2 Put the scallops into a bowl. Add the marinade and turn the scallops until they are well coated.

3 Then cover with plastic wrap and let marinate for 1 hour or overnight in the refrigerator.

4 Heat the corn oil in a wok or skillet, add the onions, and stir-fry until softened but not browned.

5 Add the tomatoes and chiles and stir-fry for 1 minute.

6 Add the scallops and stir-fry for 6–8 minutes, until the scallops are cooked through, but still succulent and tender inside.

7 Serve immediately, garnished with lime wedges.

stir-fried squid with black bean sauce

serves four

1 lb 10 oz/750 g squid, cleaned

1 large red bell pepper, seeded

1 cup snow peas

1 head bok choy

3 tbsp black bean sauce

1 tbsp Thai fish sauce

1 tbsp Chinese rice wine

1 tbsp dark soy sauce

1 tsp brown sugar

1 tsp cornstarch

1 tbsp water

1 tbsp corn oil

1 tsp sesame oil

1 fresh red bird-eye chile, chopped

1 garlic clove, chopped finely

1 tsp fresh gingerroot, grated

2 scallions, chopped

1 Cut the tentacles from the squid and discard. Cut the body cavities into fourths lengthwise. Use the tip of a small sharp knife to score a diamond pattern into the flesh, without cutting all the way through. Pat dry with paper towels.

2 Cut the bell pepper into long, thin slices. Cut the snow peas in half diagonally. Coarsely shred the bok choy.

3 Mix the black bean sauce, fish sauce, rice wine, soy sauce, and sugar. Blend the cornstarch with the water and stir into the other sauce ingredients. Set aside.

4 Heat the corn oil and sesame oil in a preheated wok. Add the chile, garlic, ginger, and scallions and stir-fry for 1 minute. Add the bell pepper and stir-fry for about 2 minutes.

5 Add the squid and stir-fry over a high heat for 1 minute. Stir in the snow peas and bok choy, and stir-fry for 1 minute, until wilted.

6 Stir in the sauce ingredients and cook, stirring constantly, for about 2 minutes, until the sauce thickens. Serve immediately.

spicy scallops with lime & chile

serves four

16 large scallops

1 tbsp butter

1 tbsp vegetable oil

1 tsp minced garlic

1 tsp grated fresh gingerroot

bunch of scallions, sliced thinly

finely grated peel of 1 lime

1 small fresh red chile, seeded and
   very finely chopped

3 tbsp lime juice

TO SERVE

lime wedges

cooked rice

1 Trim the scallops, then wash, and pat dry. Separate the corals from the white parts, then slice each white part in half horizontally, making 2 rounds.

COOK'S TIP

If fresh scallops are not available, frozen ones can be used, but make sure they are thoroughly thawed before you cook them.

2 Heat the butter and vegetable oil in a wok or skillet. Add the garlic and ginger and stir-fry for 1 minute without browning. Add the scallions and stir-fry for 1 minute.

3 Add the scallops and stir-fry over high heat for 4–5 minutes. Stir in the lime peel, chile, and lime juice and cook for 1 minute more.

4 Serve the scallops hot, with the juices spooned over them, accompanied by lime wedges and cooked rice.

crispy fried squid with salt & pepper

serves four

1 lb/450 g squid, cleaned

4 tbsp cornstarch

1 tsp salt

1 tsp pepper

1 tsp chili flakes

peanut oil

dipping sauce, to serve

COOK'S TIP

To make a dipping sauce, mix
1 tablespoon each light and dark
soy sauce, 2 teaspoons sesame
oil, 2 seeded and very finely
chopped fresh green chiles,
2 finely chopped scallions,
1 minced garlic clove, and
1 tablespoon grated fresh
gingerroot.

1 Using a sharp knife, remove the tentacles from the squid and trim. Slice the bodies down one side and open out to give a flat piece.

2 Score the flat pieces with a criss-cross pattern, then cut each piece into 4.

3 Mix the cornstarch, salt, pepper, and chili flakes.

4 Place the salt and pepper mixture in a large plastic bag. Add the squid pieces and shake the bag thoroughly to coat the squid in the flour mixture.

5 Heat about 2 inches/5 cm of peanut oil in a preheated wok.

6 Add the squid pieces to the wok, in batches, and stir-fry for about 2 minutes, or until the squid pieces start to curl up. Do not overcook or the squid will become tough and inedible.

7 Remove the squid pieces with a slotted spoon, transfer to paper towels, and drain thoroughly.

8 Transfer the fried squid pieces to serving plates and serve immediately with a dipping sauce.

whole fried fish with soy & ginger

serves four to six

6 dried shiitake mushrooms

3 tbsp rice vinegar

2 tbsp brown sugar

3 tbsp dark soy sauce

3-inch/7.5-cm fresh gingerroot,
    chopped finely

4 scallions, sliced diagonally

2 tsp cornstarch

2 tbsp lime juice

1 sea bass, about 2 lb 4 oz/
    1 kg, cleaned

4 tbsp all-purpose flour

corn oil, for deep-frying

salt and pepper

1 radish, sliced but left whole,
    to garnish

TO SERVE

shredded Napa cabbage

radish slices

1 Soak the dried mushrooms in hot water for about 10 minutes, then drain well. Set aside ½ cup of the liquid. Cut the mushrooms into thin slices.

2 Mix the reserved mushroom liquid with the rice vinegar, sugar, and soy sauce. Place in a pan with the mushrooms and bring to a boil. Reduce the heat and simmer for 3–4 minutes.

3 Add the ginger and scallions and simmer for 1 minute. Blend the cornstarch and lime juice to a smooth paste, stir into the pan, and cook, stirring, for 1–2 minutes, until the sauce thickens. Cover the sauce and set aside while you cook the fish.

4 Season the fish inside and out with salt and pepper, then dust lightly with flour, shaking off the excess.

5 Heat a 1-inch/2.5-cm depth of corn oil in a wok to 375°F/190°C, or until a cube of bread browns in 30 seconds. Carefully lower the fish into the oil and fry on 1 side for about 3–4 minutes, until golden. Use 2 metal spatulas or spoons to turn the fish carefully and fry on the other side for an additional 3–4 minutes, until golden brown all over.

6 Lift the fish out of the wok, draining off the excess oil, and place on a serving plate. Heat the sauce until boiling, then spoon it over the fish. Serve immediately, garnished with the sliced whole radish and surrounded by shredded Napa cabbage with sliced radishes.

stir-fried oysters

serves four

8 oz/225 g leeks

12 oz/350 g firm bean curd
(drained weight)

2 tbsp corn oil

12 oz/350 g shelled oysters

2 tbsp fresh lemon juice

1 tsp cornstarch

2 tbsp light soy sauce

generous ⅓ cup fish bouillon

2 tbsp chopped fresh cilantro

1 tsp finely grated lemon peel

VARIATION

Shelled clams or mussels
could be used instead of the
oysters, if you like.

1 Wash the leeks thoroughly, then trim, and slice thinly.

2 Using a sharp knife, cut the bean curd into bite-size pieces.

3 Heat the corn oil in a large preheated wok or skillet. Add the leeks to the wok or skillet and stir-fry for about 2 minutes.

4 Add the bean curd and oysters to the wok or skillet and cook for 1–2 minutes.

5 Mix the lemon juice, cornstarch, light soy sauce, and fish bouillon together in a small bowl, stirring until well blended.

6 Pour the cornstarch mixture into the wok or skillet and cook, stirring occasionally, until the juices start to thicken.

7 Transfer to serving bowls and sprinkle the cilantro and lemon peel on top. Serve immediately.

seafood chow mein

serves four

3 oz/85 g squid, cleaned

3–4 fresh scallops

3 oz/85 g raw shrimp, shelled

½ egg white, beaten lightly

2 tsp cornstarch mixed to a paste
    with 2½ tsp water

9½ oz/275 g egg noodles

5–6 tbsp vegetable oil

2 tbsp light soy sauce

¾ cup snow peas

½ tsp salt

½ tsp sugar

1 tsp Chinese rice wine

2 scallions, shredded finely

few drops of sesame oil

1 Open up the squid and score
the inside in a criss-cross pattern,
then cut into small rectangles. Soak the
squid in a bowl of boiling water until
all the pieces curl up. Rinse in cold
water and drain.

2 Cut each scallop into 3–4 slices.
Cut the shrimp in half lengthwise
if large. Mix the scallops and
shrimp with the egg white and
cornstarch paste.

3 Cook the noodles in boiling
water according to the package
instructions, then drain, and rinse
under cold water. Drain well, then toss
with about 1 tablespoon of oil.

4 Heat 3 tablespoons of oil in a
preheated wok. Add the noodles
and 1 tablespoon of the soy sauce and
stir-fry for 2–3 minutes. Transfer to a
large serving dish.

5 Heat the remaining oil in the wok
and add the snow peas and
seafood. Stir-fry for about 2 minutes,
then add the salt, sugar, rice wine,
remaining soy sauce, and about half
the scallions. Blend well and add a
little bouillon or water, if necessary.
Pour the seafood mixture on top of the
noodles and sprinkle with sesame oil.
Garnish with the remaining scallions
and serve immediately.

seafood stir-fry

serves four

3½ oz/100 g small, thin asparagus
  spears, trimmed

1 tbsp corn oil

1-inch/2.5-cm piece fresh
  gingerroot, cut into thin strips

1 leek, shredded

2 carrots, cut into very thin strips

3½ oz/100 g baby corn cobs, cut
  into fourths lengthwise

2 tbsp light soy sauce

1 tbsp oyster sauce

1 tsp honey

1 lb/450 g cooked, assorted
  shellfish, thawed if frozen

freshly cooked egg noodles,
  to serve

TO GARNISH

4 cooked jumbo shrimp

small bunch snipped fresh chives

1 Bring a small pan of water to a boil and blanch the asparagus for 1–2 minutes.

2 Drain the asparagus thoroughly and keep warm.

3 Heat the corn oil in a wok or large heavy skillet and stir-fry the ginger, leek, carrots, and baby corn cobs for about 3 minutes. Do not let the vegetables brown.

4 Add the soy sauce, oyster sauce, and honey.

5 Stir in the cooked shellfish and continue to stir-fry for 2–3 minutes until the vegetables are just tender and the shellfish are thoroughly heated through. Add the blanched asparagus and stir-fry for about 2 minutes.

6 To serve, pile the cooked noodles onto 4 warmed serving plates and spoon the seafood and vegetable stir-fry over them.

7 Garnish with the cooked shrimp and snipped fresh chives and serve immediately.

spiced balti seafood

serves four

1 garlic clove, minced

2 tsp grated fresh gingerroot

2 tsp ground coriander

2 tsp ground cumin

½ tsp ground cardamom

¼ tsp chili powder

2 tbsp tomato paste

5 tbsp water

3 tbsp chopped fresh cilantro

500 g/1 lb cooked shelled
    jumbo shrimp

2 tbsp corn oil

2 small onions, sliced

1 fresh green chile, chopped

salt

1 Put the minced garlic, grated ginger, ground coriander, cumin, cardamom, chili powder, tomato paste, 4 tablespoons of the water, and 2 tablespoons of the chopped fresh cilantro into a bowl. Mix all the ingredients together.

2 Add the shrimp to the bowl, cover with plastic wrap, and let marinate for 2 hours.

3 Heat the corn oil in a preheated wok or skillet, add the onions, and stir-fry until golden brown.

4 Add the shrimp with their marinade and the chile and stir-fry over medium heat for 5 minutes. Season with salt to taste and add the remaining tablespoon of water if the mixture is very dry. Stir-fry over medium heat for 5 minutes.

5 Serve the shrimp immediately, garnished with the remaining chopped fresh cilantro.

> **COOK'S TIP**
> Shrimp lose less flavor if they are put without water into a tightly covered pan and set over high heat to cook in their own juice.

Vegetarian Dishes

Vegetables play an important role in wok and stir-fry cooking in the Far East and are used extensively in all meals. It is perfectly possible to enjoy a meal from a selection of the following recipes contained in this chapter without meat or fish. Baby corn cobs, Napa cabbage and green beans, young spinach leaves, and bok choy can all bring a unique flavor and freshness to a stir-fried dish.

Far Eastern people enjoy their vegetables crisp, so most of the dishes in this chapter are quick to cook in order to bring out the flavors and textures of the ingredients used. Always buy firm, crisp vegetables, and cook them as soon as possible. Another point to remember is to wash the vegetables just before cutting and to cook them as soon as they have been cut so that the vitamin content is not lost.

vegetables with sherry & soy sauce

serves four

2 tbsp corn oil

1 red onion, sliced

2 carrots, sliced thinly

6 oz/175 g zucchini,
sliced diagonally

1 red bell pepper, seeded and sliced

1 small head Napa
cabbage, shredded

1½ cups bean sprouts

8 oz/225 g canned bamboo shoots,
drained and rinsed

1 cup cup cashew nuts, toasted

SAUCE

3 tbsp medium sherry

3 tbsp light soy sauce

1 tsp ground ginger

1 garlic clove, minced

1 tsp cornstarch

1 tbsp tomato paste

VARIATION

Use any mixture of fresh
vegetables that you have to hand
in this very versatile dish.

1 Heat the corn oil in a large preheated wok.

2 Add the red onion and cook for 2–3 minutes, or until softened.

3 Add the carrots, zucchini, and bell pepper slices to the wok and cook for an additional 5 minutes.

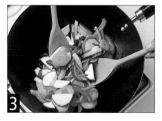

4 Add the shredded Napa cabbage, bean sprouts, and bamboo shoots to the wok and heat through for 2–3 minutes, or until the leaves start to wilt. Stir in the cashew nuts.

5 Mix the sherry, soy sauce, ginger, garlic, cornstarch, and tomato paste in a bowl. Pour over the vegetables and toss well. Let simmer for 2–3 minutes, or until the juices start to thicken. Serve immediately.

bean curd with bell peppers & onions

serves four

12 oz/350 g firm bean curd
(drained weight)

2 cloves garlic, crushed

4 tbsp dark soy sauce

1 tbsp sweet chili sauce

6 tbsp corn oil

1 onion, sliced

1 green bell pepper, seeded and diced

1 tbsp sesame oil

1 Using a sharp knife, cut the bean curd into bite size pieces. Place the bean curd cubes in a shallow, nonmetallic dish.

2 Mix the garlic, soy sauce, and sweet chili sauce and drizzle over the bean curd. Toss well to coat, cover with plastic wrap, and let marinate for about 20 minutes.

3 Meanwhile, heat the corn oil in a large preheated wok.

4 Add the onion and stir-fry over high heat until brown and crisp. Remove the onion with a slotted spoon and drain on paper towels.

5 Add the bean curd to the hot oil and stir-fry over medium heat for about 5 minutes. Stir gently to avoid breaking up the bean curd.

6 Carefully pour off all but about 1 tablespoon of the corn oil from the wok. Add the bell pepper to the wok and stir-fry for 2–3 minutes, or until softened.

7 Return the bean curd and onions to the wok and heat through, stirring occasionally.

8 Drizzle with sesame oil. Transfer the stir-fry to warmed serving plates and serve immediately.

green & black bean stir-fry

serves four

8 oz/225 g fine green beans

4 shallots

3½ oz/100 g shiitake mushrooms

1 garlic clove, minced

1 iceberg lettuce, shredded

1 tsp chili oil

2 tbsp butter

4 tbsp black bean sauce

COOK'S TIP

If possible, use Chinese green beans, which are tender and can be eaten whole. They are available from Chinese stores.

1 Using a sharp knife, slice the fine green beans, shallots, and shiitake mushrooms. Mince the garlic with a pestle and mortar and shred the iceberg lettuce.

2 Heat the chili oil and butter in a large preheated wok or skillet, swirling it over the bottom.

3 Add the green beans, shallots, garlic, and mushrooms and stir-fry for 2–3 minutes.

4 Add the shredded lettuce to the wok or skillet and stir-fry until the leaves have wilted.

5 Stir in the black bean sauce and heat through, tossing gently to mix, until the sauce is bubbling.

6 Transfer the green and black bean stir-fry to a warmed serving dish and serve immediately.

mixed vegetables in peanut sauce

serves four

2 carrots

1 small cauliflower, trimmed

2 small heads bok choy

5½ oz/150 g green beans

2 tbsp vegetable oil

1 garlic clove, chopped finely

6 scallions, sliced

1 tsp chili paste

2 tbsp soy sauce

2 tbsp Chinese rice wine

4 tbsp smooth peanut butter

3 tbsp coconut milk

COOK'S TIP

It's important to cut the
vegetables thinly into pieces
of a similar size so that they
cook quickly and evenly.
Prepare all the vegetables
before you start to cook.

1 Cut the carrots diagonally into thin slices. Cut the cauliflower into small flowerets, then slice the stalk thinly. Thickly slice the bok choy. Cut the beans into 1¼-inch/3-cm lengths.

2 Heat the oil in a preheated wok or large skillet. Add the garlic and scallions and stir-fry over medium heat for about 1 minute. Stir in the chili paste and cook for a few seconds.

3 Add the carrots and cauliflower and stir-fry for 2–3 minutes.

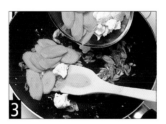

4 Add the bok choy and bean. Stir-fry for an additional 2 minutes. Stir in the soy sauce and rice wine.

5 Mix the peanut butter with the coconut milk and stir into the wok, then cook, stirring constantly, for 1 minute. Serve immediately.

balti dhal

serves four

1 cup chana dhal or yellow split
   peas, washed

½ tsp ground turmeric

1 tsp ground coriander

1 tsp salt

4 curry leaves

2 tbsp corn oil

½ tsp asafetida powder, optional

1 tsp cumin seeds

2 onions, chopped

2 garlic cloves, minced

½-inch/1-cm piece fresh
   gingerroot, grated

½ tsp garam masala

1 Put the chana dhal or yellow split peas in a large heavy pan and pour in enough water to cover by 1 inch/2.5 cm. Bring to a boil and use a metal spoon to remove the scum that has formed.

2 Add the turmeric, ground coriander, salt, and curry leaves. Reduce the heat and let simmer for 1 hour, until the chana dhal or yellow split peas are tender, but have not disintegrated. Drain well.

3 Heat the corn oil in a wok. Add the asafetida (if using) and stir-fry for 30 seconds.

4 Add the cumin seeds and stir-fry until they start popping.

5 Add the onions and stir-fry for 5 minutes, until golden brown.

6 Add the garlic, ginger, garam masala, and chana dhal or yellow split peas and stir-fry for 2 minutes. Serve the Balti dhal immediately as a side dish with a curry meal or set aside to cool, then store in the refrigerator for later use.

mixed bean stir-fry

serves four

14 oz/400 g canned red kidney beans

14 oz/400 g canned cannellini beans

6 scallions

7 oz/200 g canned pineapple rings
   or pieces in natural juice, chopped

2 tbsp pineapple juice

3–4 pieces of preserved ginger

2 tbsp ginger syrup from the jar

thinly pared peel of ½ lime or
   lemon, cut into julienne strips

2 tbsp lime or lemon juice

2 tbsp light soy sauce

1 tsp cornstarch

1 tbsp sesame oil

4 oz/115 g green beans, cut into
   1½-inch/4-cm lengths

8 oz/225 g canned bamboo shoots

salt and pepper

1 Drain the kidney and cannellini beans, rinse under cold water, and drain again.

2 Cut 4 scallions into narrow diagonal slices. Thinly slice the remainder and set aside for garnish.

3 Mix the pineapple and juice, ginger and syrup, citrus peel and juice, soy sauce, and cornstarch.

4 Heat the oil in the wok, swirling it around until really hot. Add the diagonally sliced scallions and stir-fry for about 1 minute, then add the green beans. Drain and thinly slice the bamboo shoots, add to the wok, and continue to stir-fry for 2 minutes.

5 Add the pineapple and ginger mixture and bring just to a boil. Add the canned beans and stir until very hot—for 1–2 minutes.

6 Season to taste with salt and pepper, sprinkle with the reserved chopped scallions, and serve.

chinese vegetable pancakes

serves four

1 tbsp vegetable oil

1 garlic clove, minced

1-inch/2.5-cm piece fresh
   gingerroot, grated

bunch of scallions,
   shredded lengthwise

1½ cups snow peas, shredded

8 oz/225 g bean curd
   (drained weight), cut into
   ½-inch/1-cm pieces

2 tbsp dark soy sauce, plus extra
   to serve

2 tbsp hoisin sauce, plus extra
   to serve

¾ cup canned bamboo shoots,
   drained and rinsed

2 oz/55 g canned water chestnuts,
   drained and sliced

1¾ cups bean sprouts

1 small fresh red chile, seeded and
   thinly sliced

small bunch of fresh chives

12 soft Chinese pancakes

TO SERVE

shredded Napa cabbage leaves

1 cucumber, sliced

strips of fresh red chile

1 Heat the oil in a preheated wok or a large skillet and stir-fry the garlic and ginger for 1 minute.

2 Add the scallions, snow peas, bean curd, and soy and hoisin sauces. Stir-fry for 2 minutes.

3 Add the bamboo shoots, water chestnuts, bean sprouts, and chile to the wok. Stir-fry for 2 minutes, until the vegetables are just tender.

4 Snip the fresh chives into 1-inch/2.5-cm lengths and stir them into the mixture.

5 Heat the pancakes according to the instructions on the package and keep warm.

6 Divide the vegetables and bean curd equally among the pancakes. Roll up and serve with the Napa cabbage leaves, cucumber, chile strips, and extra soy and hoisin sauces for dipping.

bean curd casserole

serves four

1 lb/450 g firm bean curd
(drained weight)

2 tbsp peanut oil

8 scallions, cut into batons

2 celery stalks, sliced

4½ oz/125 g broccoli flowerets

4½ oz/125 g zucchini, sliced

2 garlic cloves, sliced thinly

1 lb/450 g baby spinach

cooked rice, to serve

SAUCE

scant 2 cups vegetable bouillon

2 tbsp light soy sauce

3 tbsp hoisin sauce

½ tsp chili powder

1 tbsp sesame oil

1 Using a sharp knife, cut the bean curd into 1-inch/2.5-cm cubes and set aside until required.

2 Heat the peanut oil in a preheated wok or large heavy skillet, swirling it over the bottom until really hot.

3 Add the scallions, celery, broccoli, zucchini, garlic, spinach, and bean curd to the wok or skillet and stir-fry over medium heat for 3–4 minutes.

4 To make the sauce, mix the vegetable bouillon, soy sauce, hoisin sauce, chili powder, and sesame oil in a ovenproof casserole and bring to a boil.

5 Add the vegetables and bean curd, reduce the heat, cover, and let simmer for 10 minutes.

6 Transfer the bean curd and vegetables to a warmed serving dish and serve with rice.

sweet-&-sour bean curd with vegetables

serves four

2 celery stalks

1 carrot

1 green bell pepper, seeded

3 oz/85 g snow peas

2 tbsp vegetable oil

2 garlic cloves, minced

8 baby corn cobs

2 cups bean sprouts

1 lb/450 g firm bean curd (drained
weight), cubed

rice or noodles, to serve

SAUCE

2 tbsp brown sugar

2 tbsp wine vinegar

1 cup vegetable bouillon

1 tsp tomato paste

1 tbsp cornstarch

COOK'S TIP

Be careful not to break up the
bean curd cubes when stirring.

1 Using a sharp knife, thinly slice the celery, cut the carrot into thin strips, dice the bell pepper, and cut the snow peas in half diagonally.

2 Heat the vegetable oil in a preheated wok until it is almost smoking. Reduce the heat slightly, add the minced garlic, celery, carrot, bell pepper, snow peas, and baby corn cobs, and stir-fry over medium heat for 3–4 minutes.

3 Add the bean sprouts and bean curd to the wok and cook for 2 minutes, stirring frequently.

4 To make the sauce, mix the sugar, wine vinegar, bouillon, tomato paste, and cornstarch, stirring well to mix. Stir into the wok, bring to a boil, and cook, stirring constantly, until the sauce thickens. Continue to cook for 1 minute. Serve immediately with rice or noodles.

bean curd & vegetable stir-fry

serves four

1¼ cups diced potatoes

1 tbsp vegetable oil

1 red onion, sliced

8 oz/225 g firm bean curd (drained
weight), diced

2 zucchini, diced

8 canned artichoke hearts, halved

⅔ cup bottled strained tomatoes

1 tbsp sweet chili sauce

1 tbsp light soy sauce

1 tsp superfine sugar

2 tbsp chopped fresh basil

salt and pepper

1 Cook the potatoes in a pan of boiling water for 10 minutes. Drain thoroughly and set aside.

2 Heat the vegetable oil in a preheated wok or large skillet and stir-fry the red onion for 2 minutes, until the onion has softened.

3 Stir in the bean curd and zucchini and stir-fry for 3–4 minutes, until they start to brown.

4 Add the cooked potatoes to the wok or skillet, stirring to mix.

5 Stir in the artichoke hearts, bottled strained tomatoes, sweet chili sauce, soy sauce, sugar, and basil.

6 Season to taste with salt and pepper and cook for an additional 5 minutes, stirring well.

7 Transfer the bean curd and vegetable stir-fry to serving dishes and serve immediately.

COOK'S TIP

Canned artichoke hearts should be drained thoroughly and rinsed before use because they often have salt added.

crispy bean curd with chili soy sauce

serves four

10½ oz/300 g firm bean curd
  (drained weight)
2 tbsp vegetable oil
1 garlic clove, sliced
1 carrot, cut into batons
½ green bell pepper, seeded and cut
  into batons
1 fresh red bird-eye chile, seeded
  and finely chopped
3 tbsp light soy sauce
1 tbsp lime juice
1 tbsp soft light brown sugar
pickled garlic slices, to
  serve (optional)

1 Pat the bean curd dry with paper towels. Using a sharp knife, cut into ¾-inch/2-cm cubes.

2 Heat the vegetable oil in a preheated wok. Add the garlic and stir-fry over medium heat for 1 minute. Remove the garlic with a slotted spoon and add the bean curd, then cook quickly until well browned, turning gently to brown on all sides.

3 Lift out the bean curd with a slotted spoon, drain well, and keep hot. Stir the carrot and green bell pepper into the wok and stir-fry for 1 minute.

4 Spoon the carrot and bell peppers onto a warmed serving dish and pile the bean curd on top.

5 Mix together the chile, soy sauce, lime juice, and sugar, stirring until the sugar is dissolved.

6 Spoon the sauce over the bean curd and serve topped with slices of pickled garlic, if you like.

stir-fried ginger mushrooms

serves four

2 tbsp vegetable oil

3 garlic cloves, minced

1 tbsp Thai red curry paste

½ tsp ground turmeric

15 oz/425 g canned Chinese straw
   mushrooms, drained and halved

¾-inch/2-cm piece fresh gingerroot,
   shredded finely

scant ½ cup coconut milk

1½ oz/40 g dried Chinese black
   mushrooms, soaked, drained,
   and sliced

1 tbsp lemon juice

1 tbsp light soy sauce

2 tsp sugar

½ tsp salt

8 cherry tomatoes, halved

7 oz/200 g firm bean curd (drained
   weight), diced

fresh cilantro leaves, to garnish

cooked fragrant rice, to serve

1 Heat the oil in a preheated wok
   or skillet and stir-fry the garlic for
about 1 minute. Stir in the curry paste
and ground turmeric and stir-fry for
about an additional 30 seconds.

2 Stir in the straw mushrooms
   and ginger and stir-fry for about
2 minutes. Stir in the coconut milk and
bring to a boil.

3 Stir in the Chinese dried black
   mushrooms, lemon juice, soy sauce,
sugar, and salt and heat thoroughly.
Add the tomatoes and bean curd and
toss gently to heat through.

4 Sprinkle the cilantro leaves over
   the mixture and serve
immediately with fragrant rice.

spicy vegetable fritters with sweet chili dip

serves four

1 cup all-purpose flour

1 tsp ground coriander

1 tsp ground cumin

1 tsp ground turmeric

1 tsp salt

½ tsp pepper

2 garlic cloves, chopped finely

1¼-inch/3-cm piece fresh
   gingerroot, chopped

2 small fresh green chiles,
   chopped finely

1 tbsp chopped fresh cilantro

about 1 cup water

1 onion, chopped

1 potato, grated coarsely

½ cup corn kernels

1 small eggplant, diced

1 cup Chinese broccoli, cut into
   short lengths

coconut oil, for deep-frying

SWEET CHILE DIP

2 fresh red bird-eye chiles,
   chopped finely

4 tbsp superfine sugar

4 tbsp rice vinegar

1 tbsp light soy sauce

1 Make the dip by mixing the bird-eye chiles, sugar, rice vinegar, and soy sauce, mixing thoroughly until the sugar has completely dissolved. Cover with plastic wrap and let stand until needed.

2 For the fritters, place the flour in a bowl and stir in the ground coriander, cumin, turmeric, salt, and pepper. Add the garlic, ginger, green chiles, and chopped fresh cilantro with just enough cold water to make a thick batter.

3 Add the onion, potato, corn kernels, eggplant, and Chinese broccoli to the batter and stir well to distribute evenly.

4 Heat the oil in a wok to 375°F/190°C, or until a cube of bread browns in about 30 seconds. Drop tablespoons of the batter into the hot oil and cook until golden brown and crisp, turning once.

5 Keep the first batches of fritters hot in a warm oven while you are cooking the others.

6 Drain the fritters thoroughly on paper towels, and serve immediately, with the sweet chili dip.

COOK'S TIP

Chinese broccoli is also known as Chinese kale and gaai laan. The leaves are green, with a grayish white bloom.

deep-fried zucchini

serves four

1 lb/450 g zucchini
1 egg white
⅓ cup cornstarch
1 tsp salt
1 tsp Chinese five-spice powder
oil, for deep-frying
chili dip, to serve

VARIATION

Alter the seasoning by using chili powder or curry powder instead of the Chinese five-spice powder, if you like.

---

1 Using a sharp knife, slice the zucchini into either thin rings or chunky sticks.

2 Place the egg white in a small mixing bowl. Whisk lightly until foamy, using a fork.

3 Mix the cornstarch, salt, and Chinese five-spice powder and spread out the mixture on a large plate.

4 Heat the oil for deep-frying in a large preheated wok or a heavy skillet.

5 Dip each piece of zucchini into the beaten egg white, then coat thoroughly in the cornstarch and five-spice mixture.

6 Deep-fry the zucchini, in batches, for about 5 minutes, or until pale golden and crispy. Repeat with the remaining zucchini.

7 Remove the zucchini with a slotted spoon, drain on paper towels and keep warm while you are deep-frying the remainder.

8 Transfer the zucchini to warmed serving plates and serve immediately with chili dip.

deep-fried chili corn balls

serves four

6 scallions, sliced

3 tbsp chopped fresh cilantro

8 oz/225 g canned corn kernels

1 tsp mild chili powder

1 tbsp sweet chili sauce, plus extra
   to serve

¼ cup dry unsweetened coconut

1 egg

⅓ cup cornmeal

oil, for deep-frying

1 In a large bowl, mix the scallions, chopped cilantro, corn kernels, chili powder, sweet chili sauce, dry unsweetened coconut, egg, and cornmeal until well blended.

2 Cover the bowl with plastic wrap and let stand for about 10 minutes for the flavors to mingle.

3 Heat the oil for deep-frying in a large preheated wok or skillet to 375°F/190°C. or until a cube of bread browns in 30 seconds.

4 Carefully drop spoonfuls of the mixture into the hot oil. Deep-fry, in batches, for 4–5 minutes, or until crisp and a deep golden brown.

5 Remove the chili corn balls with a slotted spoon, transfer to paper towels, and drain thoroughly. Keep warm in a low oven while you cook the remaining batches.

6 Transfer the chili corn balls to serving plates and serve with extra sweet chili sauce for dipping.

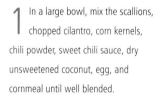

179

asparagus & red bell pepper parcels

serves four

1 red bell pepper, seeded

3½ oz/100 g fine tip asparagus

½ cup bean sprouts

2 tbsp plum sauce

1 egg yolk

8 sheets phyllo pastry

oil, for deep-frying

sweet chili dipping sauce, to serve

1 Slice the red bell pepper, and place with the asparagus and bean sprouts in a large mixing bowl.

2 Add the plum sauce to the vegetables and stir well until thoroughly mixed.

3 Beat the egg yolk and set aside until required.

4 Lay the sheets of phyllo pastry out onto a clean counter and work on 1 sheet at a time.

5 Place a little of the asparagus and red bell pepper filling at the top end of each phyllo pastry sheet. Brush the edges of the phyllo pastry with a little of the beaten egg yolk.

6 Roll up the phyllo pastry, tucking in the ends and enclosing the filling like a spring roll. Repeat with the remaining phyllo sheets.

7 Heat the oil for deep-frying in a large preheated wok. Carefully cook the parcels, 2 at a time, in the hot oil for 4–5 minutes, or until crisp.

8 Remove the parcels with a slotted spoon and let them drain on paper towels.

9 Transfer the asparagus and bell pepper parcels to serving plates and serve with the dipping sauce.

COOK'S TIP

Be sure to use fine-tipped asparagus, as it is more tender than the larger stems.

spinach stir-fry with shiitake & honey

serves four

4 scallions

3 tbsp peanut oil

12 oz/350 g shiitake
   mushrooms, sliced

2 garlic cloves, minced

12 oz/350 g baby spinach leaves

2 tbsp Chinese rice wine or
   dry sherry

2 tbsp honey

1 Using a sharp knife, thinly slice the scallions.

2 Heat the peanut oil in a preheated wok or a large heavy skillet.

3 Add the shiitake mushrooms and stir-fry over medium heat for about 5 minutes, or until the mushrooms have softened.

4 Stir the minced garlic into the wok or skillet.

5 Add the baby spinach leaves to the wok or skillet and cook for an additional 2–3 minutes, or until the spinach leaves have just wilted.

6 Mix the Chinese rice wine or dry sherry and honey in a small bowl, stirring well until thoroughly mixed.

Drizzle the wine or sherry and honey mixture over the spinach and heat through, stirring and tossing to coat the spinach leaves thoroughly in the mixture.

7 Transfer the glazed spinach and shiitake stir-fry to warmed individual serving dishes, sprinkle with the chopped scallions to garnish and serve immediately.

carrot & orange stir-fry

serves four

2 tbsp corn oil

2¼ cups grated carrots

8 oz/225 g leeks, shredded

2 oranges, peeled and segmented

2 tbsp tomato catsup

1 tbsp raw brown sugar

2 tbsp light soy sauce

½ cup chopped peanuts, to garnish

VARIATION

You could use pineapple instead of orange, if you like. If using canned pineapple, make sure that it is in natural juice not syrup as syrup will spoil the fresh taste of this dish.

1 Heat the corn oil in a large preheated wok or large heavy skillet, swirling it over the bottom until really hot.

2 Add the grated carrots and shredded leeks to the wok or skillet and stir-fry for 2–3 minutes, or until the vegetables have just softened, but not browned.

3 Reduce the heat, add the orange segments to the wok or skillet, and heat through gently, making sure that you do not break up the orange segments as you stir the mixture.

4 Mix the tomato catsup, brown sugar, and soy sauce together in a small bowl.

5 Add the tomato and sugar mixture to the wok and cook for 2 minutes.

6 Transfer the stir-fry to warmed serving bowls, sprinkle with the chopped peanuts, and serve.

vegetables with yellow bean sauce

serves four

1 eggplant

salt, for sprinkling

2 tbsp vegetable oil

3 garlic cloves, minced

4 scallions, chopped

1 small red bell pepper, seeded and
thinly sliced

4 baby corn cobs, halved
lengthwise

3 oz/85 g snow peas

7 oz/200 g Chinese mustard greens,
shredded coarsely

14½ oz/425 g canned Chinese
straw mushrooms, drained

2 cups bean sprouts

2 tbsp Chinese rice wine

2 tbsp yellow bean sauce

2 tbsp dark soy sauce

1 tsp chili sauce

1 tsp sugar

½ cup vegetable bouillon

1 tsp cornstarch

2 tsp water

1 Trim the eggplant and cut into 2-inch/5-cm long batons. Place in a strainer, sprinkle with salt, and set aside to drain for 30 minutes. Rinse in cold water and dry with paper towels.

2 Heat the vegetable oil in a wok or skillet and stir-fry the garlic, scallions, and bell pepper over high heat for 1 minute. Stir in the eggplant pieces and stir-fry for an additional 1 minute, or until softened.

3 Stir in the baby corn cobs and snow peas and stir-fry for about 1 minute. Add the mustard greens, mushrooms, and bean sprouts and stir-fry for 30 seconds.

4 Mix the rice wine, yellow bean sauce, soy sauce, chili sauce, and sugar and add to the wok or skillet with the bouillon. Bring to a boil, stirring constantly.

5 Blend the cornstarch with the water to form a smooth paste. Stir quickly into the wok or skillet and cook for 1 minute. Serve immediately.

stir-fried broccoli in hoisin sauce

serves four

14 oz/400 g broccoli

1 tbsp peanut oil

2 shallots, chopped finely

1 garlic clove, chopped finely

1 tbsp Chinese rice wine or
   dry sherry

5 tbsp hoisin sauce

¼ tsp pepper

1 tsp chili oil

2 Heat the peanut oil in a preheated wok and stir-fry the shallots and garlic over medium heat for 1–2 minutes, until golden brown.

3 Add the broccoli flowerets to the wok or skillet and stir-fry for 2 minutes. Add the Chinese rice wine or dry sherry and hoisin sauce and stir-fry for an additional 1 minute

1 Trim the broccoli and cut into small flowerets. Blanch in a small pan of boiling water for about 30 seconds, then drain well.

4 Stir in the ground black pepper and drizzle with a little chili oil just before serving. Transfer to warmed serving plates or bowls and serve the stir-fry hot.

COOK'S TIP

To make chili oil, tuck fresh red or green chiles into a jar and top up with olive oil or a light vegetable oil. Cover with a lid and let the flavor steep for at least 3 weeks before using.

thai-spiced mushrooms

serves four

8 large, flat mushrooms

3 tbsp corn oil

2 tbsp light soy sauce

1 garlic clove, minced

¾-inch/2-cm piece fresh galangal or
    fresh gingerroot, grated

1 tbsp Thai green curry paste

8 baby corn cobs, sliced

3 scallions, chopped

2 cups bean sprouts

3½ oz/100 g firm bean curd
    (drained weight), diced

2 tsp sesame seeds, toasted

TO SERVE

chopped cucumber

sliced red bell pepper

1 Remove the stems from the mushrooms and set aside. Place the caps on a cookie sheet. Mix 2 tablespoons of the corn oil with 1 tablespoon of the light soy sauce and brush all over the mushroom caps.

2 Cook the mushroom caps under a preheated broiler until golden and tender, turning them over once.

3 Meanwhile, chop the mushroom stems finely. Heat the remaining oil in a preheated wok or heavy skillet and stir-fry the stems with the garlic and galangal or ginger for 1 minute.

4 Stir in the curry paste, baby corn cobs, and scallions and stir-fry for 1 minute. Add the bean sprouts and stir-fry for 1 minute.

5 Add the diced bean curd and the remaining soy sauce, then toss lightly to heat through, without breaking up the bean curd. Spoon the mixture into the mushroom caps, dividing it evenly among them.

6 Sprinkle with the sesame seeds. Serve immediately with chopped cucumber and sliced red bell pepper.

eggplant & sesame salad

serves four

8 baby eggplant

salt, for sprinkling

2 tsp chili oil

2 tbsp light soy sauce

1 garlic clove, sliced thinly

1 fresh red bird-eye chile, seeded
   and sliced

1 tbsp corn oil

1 tsp sesame oil

1 tbsp lime juice

1 tsp soft light brown sugar

1 tbsp chopped fresh mint

1 tbsp sesame seeds, toasted

fresh mint leaves, to garnish

1 Cut the eggplant lengthwise into thin slices to within 1 inch/2.5 cm of the stem ends. Place in a strainer, sprinkling with salt between the slices and set aside to drain for about 30 minutes. Rinse thoroughly under cold running water and pat dry with paper towels.

2 Mix the chili oil and soy sauce and brush over the eggplant. Cook under a preheated hot broiler or grill over hot coals, turning them over occasionally and brushing frequently with more chili oil glaze, for 6–8 minutes, until golden brown and softened. Arrange them on a large serving platter.

3 Cook the garlic and chile in the corn oil for 1–2 minutes, until just starting to brown. Remove from the heat and add the sesame oil, lime juice, brown sugar, and any spare chili oil glaze.

4 Add the chopped mint and spoon the warm dressing over the eggplant.

5 Set aside to marinate for about 20 minutes, then sprinkle with toasted sesame seeds. Serve garnished with fresh mint leaves.

mushrooms with deep-fried bean curd

serves four

1 oz/25 g dried shiitake mushrooms

1 lb/450 g firm bean curd
   (drained weight)

4 tbsp cornstarch

oil, for deep-frying

2 garlic cloves, chopped finely

2 tsp grated fresh gingerroot

1 cup fresh or thawed frozen peas

1 Place the dried mushrooms in a large bowl. Pour over enough boiling water to cover and let stand for about 10 minutes.

2 Meanwhile, cut the bean curd into neat, bite-size cubes, using a sharp knife.

3 Place the cornstarch in a large mixing bowl.

4 Add the bean curd to the bowl and toss in the cornstarch until evenly coated.

5 Heat the oil for deep-frying in a large preheated wok.

6 Add the cubes of bean curd to the wok, in batches, and deep-fry, for 2–3 minutes, or until golden and crisp. Remove the bean curd with a slotted spoon and drain on paper towels.

7 Drain off all but 2 tablespoons of oil from the wok. Add the garlic, ginger, and soaked mushrooms to the wok and stir-fry.

8 Return the cooked bean curd to the wok and add the peas. Heat through for 1 minute, then serve hot.

broccoli & napa cabbage stir-fry

serves four

1 lb/450 g broccoli flowerets

2 tbsp corn oil

1 onion, sliced

2 garlic cloves, sliced thinly

¼ cup sliced almonds

1 head Napa cabbage, shredded

4 tbsp black bean sauce

1 Bring a large pan of water to a boil.

2 Add the broccoli flowerets to the pan and cook for 1 minute. Drain the broccoli thoroughly.

3 Meanwhile, heat the corn oil in a large preheated wok.

4 Add the onion and garlic slices to the wok and stir-fry until just starting to brown.

5 Add the drained broccoli flowerets and the sliced almonds to the wok and stir-fry over medium heat for an additional 2–3 minutes.

6 Add the shredded Napa cabbage leaves to the wok and stir-fry for an additional 2 minutes.

7 Stir in the black bean sauce, tossing to coat the vegetables thoroughly, and cook until the juices are just starting to bubble.

8 Transfer the vegetables to warmed individual serving bowls and serve immediately.

VARIATION
Use unsalted cashew nuts instead of the almonds, if you like.

squash with cashew nuts & cilantro

serves four

2 lb 4 oz/1 kg butternut
squash, peeled

3 tbsp peanut oil

1 onion, sliced

2 garlic cloves, minced

1 tsp coriander seeds

1 tsp cumin seeds

2 tbsp chopped fresh cilantro

generous ⅓ cup coconut milk

½ cup water

⅔ cup salted cashew nuts

TO GARNISH

freshly grated lime peel

fresh cilantro

lime wedges

1 Using a sharp knife, slice the butternut squash into small, bite-size cubes.

2 Heat the peanut oil in a large preheated wok.

3 Add the butternut squash, onion, and garlic to the wok and stir-fry for 5 minutes.

4 Stir in the coriander seeds, cumin seeds, and chopped cilantro and stir-fry for 1 minute.

COOK'S TIP

Coconut milk is available in cans from supermarkets and Asian stores. It is not the same as the liquid from the fresh nut.

5 Add the coconut milk and water to the wok and bring to a boil. Cover the wok and let simmer gently for 10–15 minutes, or until the squash is tender.

6 Add the cashew nuts and stir to mix well.

7 Transfer to warmed serving dishes and garnish with freshly grated lime peel, fresh cilantro, and lime wedges. Serve hot.

leeks with baby corn & yellow bean sauce

serves four

1 lb/450 g leeks

6 oz/175 g baby corn cobs

6 scallions

3 tbsp peanut oil

8 oz/225 g Napa
    cabbage, shredded

4 tbsp yellow bean sauce

COOK'S TIP
Yellow bean sauce is made from
crushed salted soybeans mixed
with flour and spices.

1 Using a sharp knife, slice the
leeks, halve the baby corn cobs
lengthwise, and thinly slice the
scallions on the diagonal.

2 Heat the peanut oil in a large
preheated wok or skillet until hot
and smoking.

3 Add the leeks, shredded Napa
cabbage, and baby corn cobs to
the wok or skillet.

4 Stir-fry the vegetables over high
heat for about 5 minutes, or until
the edges of the vegetables are just
starting to brown.

5 Add the scallions to the wok or
skillet, stirring to mix.

6 Add the yellow bean sauce to
the wok or skillet. Stir-fry the
mixture for an additional 2 minutes,
or until heated through and the
vegetables are coated in the sauce.

7 Transfer the vegetables to
warmed dishes and serve.

ginger & mixed vegetable stir-fry

serves four

1 tbsp grated fresh gingerroot

1 tsp ground ginger

1 tbsp tomato paste

2 tbsp corn oil

1 garlic clove, minced

2 tbsp light soy sauce

12 oz/350 g mycoprotein

3 small carrots, sliced

3½ oz/100 g green beans, sliced

4 celery stalks, sliced

1 red bell pepper, seeded and sliced

freshly cooked rice, to serve

1 Place the grated gingerroot, ground ginger, tomato paste, 1 tablespoon of the corn oil, garlic, soy sauce, and mycoprotein cubes in a large bowl. Mix well, stirring carefully so that you don't break up the mycoprotein cubes. Cover and let marinate for 20 minutes.

2 Heat the remaining corn oil in a large preheated wok.

3 Add the marinated mycoprotein mixture to the wok and stir-fry for about 2 minutes.

4 Add the carrots, green beans, celery, and red bell pepper and stir-fry for an additional 5 minutes.

5 Transfer the stir-fry to warmed serving dishes and serve immediately with freshly cooked rice.

COOK'S TIP

Fresh gingerroot will keep for several weeks in a cool, dry place. Gingerroot can also be kept frozen—break off lumps as needed.

bell peppers with chestnuts & garlic

serves four

8 oz/225 g leeks

oil, for deep-frying

3 tbsp peanut oil

1 yellow bell pepper, seeded and diced

1 green bell pepper, seeded and diced

1 red bell pepper, seeded and diced

7 oz/200 g canned water chestnuts,
 drained and sliced

2 garlic cloves, minced

3 tbsp light soy sauce

1 To make the garnish, thinly slice the leeks into narrow strips, using a sharp knife.

2 Heat the oil for deep-frying in a preheated wok or large skillet.

3 Add the sliced leeks to the wok or skillet and cook for 2–3 minutes, or until crisp. Set aside until required.

4 Pour off and discard the deep-frying oil and wipe out the wok or skillet with paper towels. Add the peanut oil and heat until smoking.

COOK'S TIP

Add 1 tablespoon of hoisin sauce with the soy sauce in step 6 for extra flavor and spice.

5 Add the yellow, green, and red bell peppers to the wok and stir-fry over high heat for about 5 minutes, or until they are slightly brown at the edges and softened.

6 Add the sliced water chestnuts, garlic, and light soy sauce to the wok and stir-fry all of the vegetables for an additional 2–3 minutes.

7 Spoon the bell pepper stir-fry on to warmed serving plates, garnish with the crisp leeks, and serve.

spiced eggplant stir-fry

serves four

3 tbsp peanut oil

2 onions, sliced

2 garlic cloves, chopped

2 eggplant, diced

2 fresh red chiles, seeded and very
   finely chopped

2 tbsp raw brown sugar

6 scallions, sliced

3 tbsp mango chutney

oil, for deep-frying

2 garlic cloves, sliced, to garnish

1 Heat the peanut oil in a large preheated wok or heavy skillet, swirling the oil around the bottom of the wok until it is really hot.

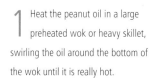

2 Add the onions and chopped garlic to the wok, stirring well.

3 Add the diced eggplant and chiles to the wok and stir-fry for 5 minutes.

4 Add the raw brown sugar, scallions, and mango chutney to the wok, stirring well.

5 Reduce the heat, cover, and let simmer, stirring from time to time, for 15 minutes, or until the eggplant are tender.

6 Transfer the stir-fry to serving bowls and keep warm.

7 Heat the oil for deep-frying in the wok and quickly cook the slices of garlic, until they brown slightly. Garnish the stir-fry with the deep-fried garlic and serve immediately.

COOK'S TIP

The "hotness" of chiles varies enormously so always use with caution, but as a general guide the smaller they are the hotter they will be. The seeds and membrane are the hottest part and are usually discarded.

vegetable stir-fry

serves four

3 tbsp vegetable oil

8 pearl onions, halved

1 eggplant, diced

8 oz/225 g zucchini, sliced

8 oz/225 g open-cap
  mushrooms, halved

2 garlic cloves, minced

14 oz/400 g canned
  chopped tomatoes

2 tbsp sun-dried tomato paste

2 tbsp soy sauce

1 tsp sesame oil

1 tbsp Chinese rice wine or
  dry sherry

pepper

fresh basil leaves, to garnish

COOK'S TIP

Basil has a very strong flavor,
which is perfect with vegetables
and Chinese flavorings. Instead
of using basil simply as a garnish
in this dish, try adding a handful
of fresh basil leaves to the
stir-fry in step 4.

1 Heat the vegetable oil in a large
preheated wok or skillet.

2 Add the pearl onions and
eggplant to the wok or skillet
and stir-fry for 5 minutes, or until the
vegetables are golden and just
starting to soften.

3 Add the sliced zucchini,
mushrooms, garlic, chopped
tomatoes, and sun-dried tomato
paste to the wok and stir-fry for about
5 minutes. Reduce the heat and let
simmer for 10 minutes, or until the
vegetables are tender, but not soft.

4 Add the soy sauce, sesame oil,
and rice wine or sherry to the
wok, bring back to a boil, and cook
for 1 minute.

5 Season the vegetable stir-fry with
pepper to taste and sprinkle with
whole basil leaves. Transfer to warmed
serving plates and serve immediately.

potato stir-fry

serves four

2 lb/900 g waxy potatoes

2 tbsp vegetable oil

1 yellow bell pepper, seeded
and diced

1 red bell pepper, seeded and diced

1 carrot, cut into thin strips

1 zucchini, cut into thin strips

2 garlic cloves, minced

1 fresh red chile, seeded and sliced

bunch of scallions, halved lengthwise

½ cup coconut milk

1 tsp chopped lemongrass

2 tsp lime juice

finely grated peel of 1 lime

1 tbsp chopped fresh cilantro

COOK'S TIP

Check that the potatoes are
not overcooked in step 2,
otherwise the potato pieces
will disintegrate when they
are stir-fried in the wok.

1 Using a sharp knife, cut the
potatoes into small dice.

2 Bring a large pan of water to the
boil and cook the diced potatoes
for 5 minutes. Drain thoroughly.

3 Heat the vegetable oil in a
preheated wok or large skillet,
swirling the oil around the bottom of
the wok or skillet until it is really hot.

4 Add the potatoes, diced bell
peppers, carrot, zucchini, garlic,
and chile to the wok or skillet, and stir-
fry the vegetables over medium heat
for 2–3 minutes.

5 Stir in the scallions, coconut milk,
chopped lemongrass, and lime
juice, and stir-fry the mixture for an
additional 5 minutes.

6 Add the lime peel and chopped
cilantro and stir-fry for 1 minute.
Serve immediately.

vegetable stir-fry with eggs

serves four

2 eggs

3 small carrots

12 oz/350 g white cabbage

2 tbsp vegetable oil

1 red bell pepper, seeded and
thinly sliced

1½ cups bean sprouts

1 tbsp tomato catsup

2 tbsp light soy sauce

½ cup salted peanuts, chopped

1 Bring a small pan of water to a
boil. Add the eggs to the pan and
cook for about 7 minutes. Remove the
eggs from the pan and cool under cold
running water for 1 minute. When cool
enough to handle, peel the shells from
the eggs, then cut the hard-cooked
eggs into fourths.

2 Peel and coarsely grate the carrots
by hand or in a food processor.

3 Remove any outer leaves from
the white cabbage and cut out
the stem, then shred the leaves very
finely, either with a sharp knife or
by using the fine slicing blade on a
food processor.

4 Heat the vegetable oil in a large
preheated wok or large skillet.

5 Add the carrots, white cabbage,
and bell pepper to the wok or
skillet and stir-fry for 3 minutes.

6 Add the bean sprouts and stir-fry
for 2 minutes.

7 Mix the tomato catsup and
soy sauce in a small bowl and
add to the wok or skillet. Add the
chopped peanuts and stir-fry for
1 minute.

8 Transfer the vegetable stir-fry to
warmed individual serving plates
and garnish with the hard-cooked egg
fourths. Serve immediately.

bok choy with red onions & cashew nuts

serves four

2 red onions

6 oz/175 g red cabbage

2 tbsp peanut oil

8 oz/225 g bok choy

2 tbsp plum sauce

²/₃ cup roasted cashew nuts

VARIATION

Use unsalted peanuts instead of the cashew nuts, if you like. You could substitute Chinese spinach, also known as callaloo, or Chinese flat cabbage for the bok choy.

1 Using a sharp knife, cut the red onions into thin wedges and thinly shred the red cabbage.

2 Heat the peanut oil in a large preheated wok or heavy skillet until it is really hot.

3 Add the onion wedges to the wok or skillet and stir-fry for about 5 minutes, or until they are just starting to brown.

4 Add the shredded red cabbage to the wok or skillet and stir-fry for an additional 2–3 minutes.

5 Add the bok choy leaves to the wok or skillet and stir-fry for about 2–3 minutes, or until the leaves have just wilted.

6 Drizzle the plum sauce over the vegetables, toss together until well mixed, and heat until the liquid is bubbling.

7 Sprinkle with the roasted cashew nuts and transfer to warmed serving bowls. Serve immediately.

nut & vegetable stir-fry

serves four

1 cup unsalted roasted peanuts

2 tsp hot chili sauce

¾ cup coconut milk

2 tbsp dark soy sauce

1 tbsp ground coriander

pinch of ground turmeric

1 tbsp molasses sugar

3 tbsp peanut oil

3–4 shallots, sliced thinly

1 garlic clove, sliced thinly

1–2 fresh red chiles, seeded and
   finely chopped

1 large carrot, cut into fine strips

1 yellow bell pepper, seeded
   and sliced

1 red bell pepper, seeded and sliced

1 zucchini, cut into fine strips

4 oz/115 g sugar snap peas, trimmed

3-inch/7.5-cm piece of cucumber,
   cut into strips

9 oz/250 g oyster mushrooms,

9 oz/250 g canned chestnuts, drained

2 tsp grated fresh gingerroot

finely grated peel and juice of 1 lime

1 tbsp chopped fresh cilantro

salt and pepper

lime slices, to garnish

1 To make the peanut sauce, grind the peanuts in a blender or chop very finely. Put into a small pan with the hot chili sauce, coconut milk, soy sauce, ground coriander, ground turmeric, and molasses sugar. Set over low heat and let simmer gently for 3–4 minutes. Keep warm and set aside until required.

2 Heat the peanut oil in a wok or large heavy skillet. Add the shallots, garlic, and chiles and stir-fry over medium heat for 2 minutes.

3 Add the carrot, bell peppers, zucchini, and sugar snap peas and stir-fry for an additional 2 minutes.

4 Add the cucumber, mushrooms, chestnuts, ginger, lime peel and juice, and chopped cilantro and stir-fry briskly for about 5 minutes, or until the vegetables are crisp, yet still crunchy. Season to taste with salt and pepper.

5 Divide the stir-fry among 4 warmed serving plates and garnish with slices of lime. Transfer the peanut sauce to a serving bowl and serve immediately with the vegetables.

long beans with tomatoes

serves four

1 lb 2 oz/500 g green beans, cut
   into 2-inch/5-cm lengths

2 tbsp vegetable ghee

1-inch/2.5-cm piece fresh
   gingerroot, grated

1 garlic clove, minced

1 tsp ground turmeric

½ tsp cayenne pepper

1 tsp ground coriander

4 tomatoes, peeled, seeded,
   and diced

⅔ cup vegetable bouillon

1 Blanch the beans briefly in boiling water, drain, refresh under cold running water, and drain again.

2 Melt the ghee in a preheated wok or pan over medium heat. Add the ginger and minced garlic, stir, and add the turmeric, cayenne, and ground coriander. Stir over low heat for about 1 minute, until fragrant.

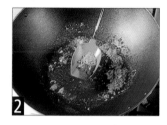

3 Add the diced tomatoes, tossing them until they are thoroughly coated in the spice mix.

4 Add the vegetable bouillon to the wok or pan, bring to a boil, and let simmer gently over medium-high heat, stirring occasionally, for about 10 minutes, until the sauce has reduced and thickened.

5 Add the beans, reduce the heat to medium, and heat through, stirring constantly, for 5 minutes.

6 Transfer to a warmed serving dish and serve immediately.

zucchini curry

serves four

6 tbsp vegetable oil

1 onion, chopped finely

3 fresh green chiles, chopped finely

1 tsp finely chopped fresh
gingerroot

1 tsp minced garlic

1 tsp chili powder

1 lb 2 oz/500 g zucchini,
sliced thinly

2 tomatoes, sliced

1 tbsp fresh cilantro leaves, plus
extra to garnish

2 tsp fenugreek seeds

chapatis, to serve

1 Heat the vegetable oil in a preheated wok or skillet. Add the onion, chiles, ginger, garlic, and chili powder and stir-fry over low heat for about 2–3 minutes, until the onion is just starting to soften.

2 Add the zucchini and the tomatoes and stir-fry over medium heat for 5–7 minutes.

3 Add the cilantro leaves and fenugreek seeds to the wok or skillet and stir-fry over medium heat for 5 minutes, until the vegetables are tender.

VARIATION
You could use coriander seeds instead of the fenugreek seeds, if you like.

4 Remove the wok or skillet from the heat and transfer the zucchini and fenugreek seed mixture to warmed serving dishes. Garnish with cilantro leaves and serve hot with chapatis.

green stir-fry

2 tbsp peanut oil

2 garlic cloves, minced

½ tsp ground star anise

1 tsp salt

12 oz/350 g bok choy, shredded

8 oz/225 g baby spinach

1 oz/25 g snow peas

1 celery stalk, sliced

1 green bell pepper, seeded
    and sliced

¼ cup vegetable bouillon

1 tsp sesame oil

COOK'S TIP

Star anise is an important
ingredient in Chinese cuisine.
The attractive star-shaped pods
are often used whole to add a
decorative garnish to dishes.
The flavor is similar to licorice,
but with spicy undertones
and is quite strong.

---

1 Heat the peanut oil in a
preheated wok or large skillet,
swirling it around the bottom until it
is really hot.

2 Add the minced garlic and
stir-fry over medium heat for
about 30 seconds. Stir in the ground
star anise, salt, shredded bok choy,
spinach, snow peas, celery, and green
bell pepper and stir-fry for 3–4 minutes.

3 Add the vegetable bouillon,
reduce the heat, cover the wok
or skillet, and cook for 3–4 minutes.
Remove the lid and stir in the sesame
oil. Mix thoroughly.

4 Transfer the green vegetable stir-
fry to a warmed serving dish and
serve immediately.

seasonal stir-fry

serves four

1 red bell pepper, seeded

4 oz/115 g zucchini

4 oz/115 g cauliflower

4 oz/115 g green beans

3 tbsp vegetable oil

a few small slices of
    fresh gingerroot

½ tsp salt

½ tsp sugar

1–2 tbsp vegetable bouillon or
    water (optional)

1 tbsp light soy sauce

a few drops of sesame oil (optional)

1 Using a sharp knife or Chinese cleaver, cut the red bell pepper into small squares. Thinly slice the zucchini. Trim the cauliflower and divide into small flowerets, discarding any thick stems. Make sure the vegetables are cut into similar shapes and sizes so that they will cook evenly. Trim the green beans, then cut them in half.

2 Heat the vegetable oil in a preheated wok or large heavy skillet. Add the prepared vegetables with the ginger and stir-fry for about 2 minutes.

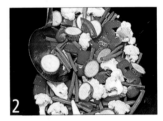

3 Add the salt and sugar to the wok or skillet and continue to stir-fry for 1–2 minutes, adding a little vegetable bouillon or water if the mixture appears to be too dry. Do not add any liquid unless necessary.

4 Add the light soy sauce and sesame oil (if using) and stir well to coat the vegetables lightly.

5 Transfer the stir-fried vegetables to a warmed serving dish or bowl and serve immediately

medley of summer vegetables

serves four

8 oz/225 g baby carrots

4½ oz/125 g string beans or
   green beans

2 zucchini

bunch of large scallions

bunch of radishes

4 tbsp butter

2 tbsp light olive oil

2 tbsp white wine vinegar

4 tbsp dry white wine

1 tsp superfine sugar

1 tbsp chopped fresh tarragon

salt and pepper

fresh tarragon sprigs,
   to garnish

3 Meanwhile, pour the olive oil, vinegar, and white wine into a small pan and add the sugar. Place over low heat, stirring until the sugar has completely dissolved. Remove the pan from the heat, then stir in the chopped tarragon.

4 When the vegetables are just cooked, pour over the dressing. Stir through, tossing the vegetables well to coat. Season to taste with salt and pepper, then transfer to a warmed serving dish. Garnish with fresh tarragon sprigs and serve the medley immediately.

1 Cut the carrots in half lengthwise, slice the beans and zucchini, and halve the scallions and radishes, so that all the vegetables are cut to even-size pieces.

2 Melt the butter in a wok or large heavy skillet. Add the carrots, beans, zucchini, scallions, and radishes and cook them over medium heat, stirring frequently, until they are tender, but still crisp and firm to the bite.

ginger & orange broccoli

serves four

1 lb 10 oz/750 g broccoli

2 thin slices fresh gingerroot

2 garlic cloves

1 orange

2 tsp cornstarch

1 tbsp light soy sauce

½ tsp sugar

2 tbsp vegetable oil

VARIATION

This dish could be made
with cauliflower, if you prefer,
or a mixture of cauliflower
and broccoli.

---

1 Divide the broccoli into small flowerets. Peel the stems, using a swivel-blade vegetable peeler, then cut the stems into thin slices, using a sharp knife.

2 Cut the gingerroot into fine slices and slice the garlic.

3 Peel 2 long strips of peel from the orange and cut into thin strips. Place the strips in a bowl, cover with cold water, and set aside.

4 Squeeze the juice from the orange and stir in the cornstarch, light soy sauce, sugar, and 4 tablespoons water until well mixed and smooth.

5 Heat the vegetable oil in a preheated wok or skillet. Add the broccoli stem and stir-fry for 2 minutes.

6 Add the ginger slices, garlic, and broccoli flowerets and stir-fry for an additional 3 minutes.

7 Stir the orange and soy sauce sauce mixture into the wok and cook, stirring constantly, until the sauce has thickened and coated the broccoli.

8 Drain the reserved orange peel and stir into the wok. Transfer to a serving dish and serve immediately.

Rice & Noodles

Rice and noodles are staple ingredients in the Far East, as they are cheap, plentiful, nutritious, and delicious. They are extremely versatile and are therefore always served as part of a meal. Many rice and noodle dishes are served as accompaniments and others as main dishes combined with meat, vegetables, and fish, all flavored with fragrant spices and seasonings.

Plain rice is served to accompany a large meal and help settle the stomach between rich, spicy courses. Noodles vary from country to country and are eaten in various forms. Thin egg noodles are made from wheat flour, water, and egg and are probably the most common in the Western diet. Available fresh or dried, they require very little cooking and are perfect for quick and easy meals.

chinese fried rice

serves four

3 cups water

1½ cups long-grain rice

2 eggs

4 tsp cold water

3 tbsp corn oil

4 scallions, diagonally sliced

1 red, green or yellow bell pepper,
   seeded and thinly sliced

3–4 lean bacon strips, rinded and
   cut into strips

3½ cups fresh bean sprouts

¼ cup frozen peas, thawed

2 tbsp light soy sauce (optional)

salt and pepper

1 Pour the water into a wok with ½ teaspoon salt and bring to a boil. Rinse the rice under cold water until the water runs clear, drain well, and add to the boiling water. Stir well, then cover the wok tightly with the lid, and let simmer for 12–13 minutes. (Don't remove the lid during cooking or the steam will escape and the rice will not be cooked.)

2 Remove the lid, stir the rice, and spread out on a large plate or cookie sheet to cool and dry.

3 Beat each egg separately with salt and pepper and 2 teaspoons of cold water. Heat 1 tablespoon of the oil in the wok, pour in the first egg, swirl it around, and cook, undisturbed, until set. Remove to a board and cook the second egg. Cut the omelets into thin slices.

4 Add the remaining oil to the wok, add the scallions and bell pepper, and stir-fry for 1–2 minutes. Add the bacon and continue to stir-fry for an additional 1–2 minutes. Add the bean sprouts and peas and toss together thoroughly. Stir in the soy sauce (if using).

5 Add the rice and seasoning and stir-fry for about 1 minute, then add the strips of omelet, and continue to stir for about 2 minutes, or until the rice is piping hot. Transfer to a warmed serving dish and serve immediately.

chinese risotto

serves four

2 tbsp peanut oil

1 onion, sliced

2 garlic cloves, minced

1 tsp Chinese five-spice powder

8 oz/225 g Chinese sausage, sliced

3 small carrots, diced

1 green bell pepper, seeded and diced

1⅓ cups risotto rice

3½ cups vegetable or chicken bouillon

6 fresh chives

COOK'S TIP

Chinese sausage is highly
flavored and is made from
chopped pork fat, pork meat,
and spices. Use a spicy
Portuguese sausage if Chinese
sausage is unavailable.

1 Heat the peanut oil in a large
preheated wok or heavy skillet,
swirling it over the bottom.

2 Add the onion slices, minced
garlic, and Chinese five-spice
powder to the wok or skillet and
stir-fry for 1 minute.

3 Add the Chinese sausage, carrots,
and green bell pepper to the wok
or skillet and stir to mix.

4 Stir in the risotto rice and cook
for 1 minute.

5 Gradually add the vegetable or
chicken bouillon, a little at a time,
stirring constantly, until the liquid has
been completely absorbed and the rice
grains are tender.

6 Snip the chives with a pair of
clean kitchen scissors and stir into
the wok with the last of the bouillon.

7 Transfer the Chinese risotto to
warmed individual serving bowls
and serve immediately.

coconut rice

serves four

1⅓ cups long-grain white rice

2½ cups water

½ tsp salt

generous ⅓ cup coconut milk

¼ cup dry unsweetened coconut

coconut shavings, to garnish

1 Rinse the rice thoroughly under cold running water until the water runs completely clear.

2 Drain the rice thoroughly in a strainer set over a large bowl. This is to remove some of the starch and to prevent the grains from sticking together during cooking.

3 Place the rice in a wok with the water.

4 Add the salt and coconut milk to the wok and bring to a boil.

5 Cover the wok with a lid or a lid made of foil, curved into a domed shape and resting on the sides of the wok. Reduce the heat and let simmer for 10 minutes.

6 Remove the lid and fluff up the rice with a fork. The liquid should be absorbed and the rice grains should be tender. If not, add more water and let simmer for a few more minutes, until all the liquid has been absorbed.

7 Spoon the rice into a warmed serving bowl and sprinkle with the dry unsweetened coconut. Garnish and serve the coconut rice immediately.

COOK'S TIP

Coconut milk is made from the white coconut flesh soaked in water and milk, then squeezed to extract all of the flavor. You can make your own or buy it in cans.

crab congee

serves four

generous 1 cup short-grain rice

6¼ cups fish bouillon

½ tsp salt

3½ oz/100 g Chinese sausage,
   sliced thinly

8 oz/225 g white crab meat

6 scallions, sliced

2 tbsp chopped fresh cilantro

pepper, to serve

COOK'S TIP

Always buy the freshest possible
crab meat; fresh is best, although
frozen or canned will work for
this recipe. In the West, crabs
are almost always sold ready-
cooked. The crab should feel
heavy for its size, and when it is
shaken, there should be no
sound of water inside.

1 Place the short-grain rice in a
large preheated wok or skillet.

2 Add the fish bouillon to the wok
or skillet and bring to a boil.

3 Reduce the heat, then let simmer
gently for 1 hour, stirring the
mixture from time to time.

4 Add the salt, sliced Chinese
sausage, white crab meat, sliced
scallions, and chopped fresh cilantro
to the wok or skillet and heat through
for about 5 minutes.

5 Add a little more water to the
wok if the congee "porridge" is
too thick, stirring well.

6 Transfer the crab congee to
warmed serving bowls, sprinkle
with pepper, and serve immediately.

stir-fried onion rice with five-spice chicken

serves four

1 tbsp Chinese five-spice powder

2 tbsp cornstarch

12 oz/350 g skinless, boneless
   chicken breast portions, diced

3 tbsp peanut oil

1 onion, diced

generous 1 cup long-grain white rice

½ tsp ground turmeric

2½ cups chicken bouillon

2 tbsp snipped fresh chives

COOK'S TIP
Be careful when using
turmeric as it can stain the
hands and clothes a
distinctive shade of yellow.

1 Place the Chinese five-spice
powder and cornstarch in a large
bowl. Add the chicken pieces and toss
to coat all over.

2 Heat 2 tablespoons of the peanut
oil in a large preheated wok. Add
the chicken to the wok and stir-fry for
5 minutes. Using a slotted spoon,
remove the chicken and set aside.

3 Add the remaining peanut oil to
the wok.

4 Add the onion to the wok and
stir-fry for 1 minute.

5 Add the rice, turmeric, and
chicken bouillon to the wok and
gently bring to a boil.

6 Return the chicken pieces to the
wok, reduce the heat, and let
simmer gently for about 10 minutes, or
until the liquid has been absorbed and
the rice is tender.

7 Add the snipped fresh chives,
stir to mix, and serve hot.

egg-fried rice with seven-spice beef

serves four

generous 1 cup long-grain white rice

2½ cups water

12 oz/350 g beef tenderloin

2 tbsp dark soy sauce

2 tbsp tomato catsup

1 tbsp seven-spice seasoning

2 tbsp peanut oil

1 onion, diced

3 small carrots, diced

1 cup frozen peas

2 eggs, beaten

2 tbsp cold water

VARIATION

You can use pork tenderloin or chicken instead of the beef, if you like.

1 Rinse the rice under cold running water, then drain thoroughly. Place the rice in a pan with the water, bring to a boil, cover, and let simmer for 12 minutes. Turn the cooked rice out onto a cookie sheet and let cool.

2 Using a sharp knife, thinly slice the beef tenderloin and place in a large, shallow dish.

3 Mix the soy sauce, tomato catsup, and seven-spice seasoning. Spoon over the beef and toss well to coat.

4 Heat the peanut oil in a preheated wok. Add the beef and stir-fry for 3–4 minutes.

5 Add the onion, carrots, and peas to the wok and stir-fry for an additional 2–3 minutes. Add the cooked rice to the wok and stir.

6 Beat the eggs with 2 tablespoons of cold water. Drizzle the egg mixture over the rice and stir-fry for 3–4 minutes, or until the rice is heated through and the egg has set. Transfer the rice and beef to a warmed serving bowl and serve immediately.

chinese chicken rice

serves four

1¾ cups long-grain white rice

1 tsp ground turmeric

2 tbsp corn oil

12 oz/350 g skinless, boneless
    chicken thighs, sliced

1 red bell pepper, seeded and sliced

1 green bell pepper, seeded and sliced

1 fresh green chile, seeded and
    finely chopped

1 carrot, grated coarsely

1½ cups bean sprouts

6 scallions, sliced, plus extra
    to garnish

2 tbsp light soy sauce

salt

1 Place the rice and turmeric in a large pan of lightly salted water and cook until the grains of rice are just tender, about 10 minutes. Drain the rice thoroughly and press out any excess water with paper towels.

2 Heat the corn oil in a large preheated wok or skillet.

3 Add the strips of chicken to the wok or skillet and stir-fry over high heat until the chicken is just starting to turn a golden color.

4 Add the sliced bell peppers and green chile to the wok and stir-fry for 2–3 minutes.

5 Add the cooked rice to the wok, a little at a time, tossing well after each addition until well mixed and the grains of rice are separated.

6 Add the carrot, bean sprouts, and scallions to the wok and stir-fry for an additional 2 minutes.

7 Drizzle with the soy sauce and toss to mix.

8 Transfer the Chinese chicken rice to a warmed serving dish, garnish with extra scallions, if you like, and serve immediately.

stir-fried rice with egg strips

serves four

2 tbsp peanut oil

1 egg, beaten with 1 tsp water

1 garlic clove, chopped finely

1 small onion, chopped finely

1 tbsp Thai red curry paste

1¼ cups long-grain rice, cooked

½ cup cooked peas

1 tbsp Thai fish sauce

2 tbsp tomato catsup

2 tbsp chopped fresh cilantro

TO GARNISH

fresh red chile flowers

cucumber slices

1 To make chile flowers for the garnish, hold the stem of each chile with your fingertips and use a small sharp, pointed knife to cut a slit down the length from near the stem end to the tip. Turn the chile about a quarter turn and make another cut. Repeat to make a total of 4 cuts, then scrape out the seeds. Cut each "petal" again, in half or into fourths, to make 8–16 petals. Place the chile in ice water.

2 Heat about 1 teaspoon of the oil in a wok. Pour in the egg mixture, swirling it to coat the pan evenly and make a thin layer. When set and golden, remove the egg from the pan and roll up. Set aside.

3 Add the remaining oil to the wok and stir-fry the garlic and onion for 1 minute. Add the curry paste, then stir in the rice and peas. Stir until heated through.

4 Stir in the fish sauce, catsup, and cilantro. Remove the wok from the heat and pile the rice into a warmed serving dish.

5 Slice the egg roll into spiral strips, without unrolling, and use to garnish the rice. Add the cucumber slices and chile flowers. Serve hot.

stir-fried rice with chinese sausage

serves four

12 oz/350 g Chinese sausage

2 tbsp corn oil

2 tbsp dark soy sauce

1 onion, sliced

2 carrots, cut into thin sticks

1¾ cups peas

¾ cup canned pineapple
   cubes, drained

4¾ cups cooked long-grain rice

1 egg, beaten

1 tbsp chopped fresh parsley

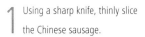

1 Using a sharp knife, thinly slice the Chinese sausage.

2 Heat the corn oil in a large preheated wok. Add the sausage to the wok and stir-fry for 5 minutes.

3 Stir in the soy sauce and let bubble for about 2–3 minutes, or until the mixture is syrupy.

4 Add the onion, carrots, peas, and pineapple to the wok and stir-fry for an additional 3 minutes.

5 Add the cooked rice to the wok and stir-fry the mixture for about 2–3 minutes, or until the rice is completely heated through.

6 Drizzle the beaten egg over the top of the rice and cook, tossing the ingredients in the wok, until the egg sets.

7 Transfer the stir-fried rice to a large, warmed serving bowl and sprinkle with plenty of chopped fresh parsley. Serve immediately.

sweet chili pork fried rice

serves four

1 lb/450 g pork tenderloin

2 tbsp corn oil

2 tbsp sweet chili sauce, plus extra
   to serve (optional)

1 onion, sliced

2 carrots, cut into thin sticks

6 oz/175 g zucchini, cut into
   thin sticks

1 cup canned bamboo shoots,
   drained and rinsed

4¾ cups cooked long-grain rice

1 egg, beaten

1 tbsp chopped fresh parsley

COOK'S TIP

For a really quick dish, add
frozen mixed vegetables to the
rice instead of the freshly
prepared vegetables.

1 Using a sharp knife, cut the pork tenderloin into thin slices.

2 Heat the corn oil in a large preheated wok or skillet.

3 Add the pork to the wok and stir-fry for 5 minutes.

4 Add the chili sauce to the wok and let bubble, stirring constantly, for 2–3 minutes, or until syrupy.

5 Add the onion, carrots, zucchini, and bamboo shoots to the wok and stir-fry for an additional 3 minutes.

6 Add the cooked rice and stir-fry for 2–3 minutes, or until the rice is heated through.

7 Drizzle the beaten egg over the top of the fried rice and cook, tossing the ingredients in the wok with 2 spoons, until the egg sets.

8 Sprinkle with chopped fresh parsley and serve immediately, with extra sweet chili sauce, if you like.

noodle salad with coconut & lime dressing

serves four

8 oz/225 g dried egg noodles

2 tsp sesame oil

1 carrot

2 cups bean sprouts

½ cucumber

2 scallions, shredded finely

5½ oz/150 g cooked turkey breast
meat, shredded into thin slivers

DRESSING

5 tbsp coconut milk

3 tbsp lime juice

1 tbsp light soy sauce

2 tsp Thai fish sauce

1 tsp chili oil

1 tsp sugar

2 tbsp chopped fresh cilantro

2 tbsp chopped fresh sweet basil

TO GARNISH

peanuts

chopped fresh basil

1 Cook the noodles in boiling water for 4 minutes, or according to the package instructions. Plunge them into a bowl of cold water to prevent any further cooking, then drain, and toss in sesame oil.

2 Use a vegetable peeler to shave off thin ribbons from the carrot. Blanch the ribbons and bean sprouts in boiling water for 30 seconds, then plunge into cold water for 30 seconds. Drain well. Shave thin ribbons of cucumber with the vegetable peeler.

3 Place the carrots, bean sprouts, cucumber, scallions, and turkey in a large bowl. Add the noodles and toss thoroughly to mix.

4 Place all the dressing ingredients in a screw-top jar and shake vigorously to mix evenly.

5 Add the dressing to the noodle mixture and toss. Pile the salad onto a serving dish. Sprinkle with peanuts and basil. Serve cold.

egg noodles with chicken & oyster sauce

serves four

9 oz/250 g egg noodles

1 lb/450 g boneless chicken thighs

2 tbsp peanut oil

1 large carrot, sliced

3 tbsp oyster sauce

2 eggs

3 tbsp cold water

VARIATION

Flavor the eggs with soy sauce or hoisin sauce as an alternative to the oyster sauce, if you like.

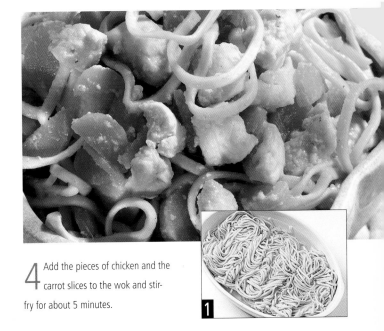

1 Place the egg noodles in a large bowl or dish. Pour over enough boiling water to cover the noodles and let stand for 10 minutes.

2 Meanwhile, remove the skin from the chicken thighs. Cut the chicken flesh into small pieces, using a sharp knife.

3 Heat the peanut oil in a large preheated wok or skillet, swirling the oil around the bottom of the wok until it is really hot.

4 Add the pieces of chicken and the carrot slices to the wok and stir-fry for about 5 minutes.

5 Drain the noodles thoroughly. Add the noodles to the wok and stir-fry for 2–3 minutes, or until the noodles are heated through.

6 Beat together the oyster sauce, eggs, and cold water. Drizzle the mixture over the noodles and stir-fry for an additional 2–3 minutes, or until the eggs have just set.

7 Transfer the mixture in the wok to warmed individual serving bowls and serve hot.

ginger chile beef with crispy noodles

serves four

8 oz/225 g medium egg noodles

12 oz/350 g beef tenderloin

2 tbsp corn oil

1 tsp ground ginger

1 garlic clove, minced

1 fresh red chile, seeded and very
   finely chopped

1 large carrot, cut into thin sticks

6 scallions, sliced

2 tbsp lime marmalade

2 tbsp dark soy sauce

oil, for deep-frying

1 Place the noodles in a large dish or bowl. Pour over enough boiling water to cover the noodles and let stand for about 10 minutes while you cook the rest of the ingredients.

2 Using a sharp knife, thinly slice the beef tenderloin.

3 Heat the corn oil in a large preheated wok or skillet.

4 Add the beef and ground ginger to the wok or skillet and stir-fry for about 5 minutes.

5 Add the minced garlic, chopped red chile, carrot sticks, and scallions to the wok and stir-fry for an additional 2–3 minutes.

6 Add the lime marmalade and soy sauce to the wok and let bubble for 2 minutes. Remove the chili beef and ginger mixture, set aside, and keep warm until required.

7 Heat the oil for deep-frying in the wok or skillet.

8 Drain the noodles thoroughly and pat dry with paper towels. Carefully lower the noodles into the hot oil and cook for 2–3 minutes, or until crisp. Drain the noodles on paper towels.

9 Divide the noodles among 4 warmed serving plates and top with the chile beef and ginger mixture. Serve immediately.

singapore-style shrimp noodles

serves four

9 oz/250 g thin rice noodles

4 tbsp peanut oil

2 garlic cloves, minced

2 fresh red chiles, seeded and very
    finely chopped

1 tsp grated fresh gingerroot

2 tbsp Madras curry paste

2 tbsp rice wine vinegar

1 tbsp superfine sugar

8 oz/225 g cooked ham,
    shredded finely

3½ oz/100 g canned water
    chestnuts, sliced

100 g/3½ oz mushrooms, sliced

¾ cup peas

1 red bell pepper, seeded and
    thinly sliced

3½ oz/100 g cooked shelled shrimp

2 extra large eggs

4 tbsp coconut milk

¼ cup dry unsweetened coconut

2 tbsp chopped fresh cilantro

1 Place the rice noodles in a large bowl, cover with boiling water, and let soak for about 10 minutes. Drain the noodles thoroughly, then toss with 2 tablespoons of peanut oil.

2 Heat the remaining peanut oil in a large preheated wok until the oil is really hot.

3 Add the garlic, chiles, ginger, curry paste, rice wine vinegar, and superfine sugar to the wok and stir-fry for 1 minute.

4 Add the ham, water chestnuts, mushrooms, peas, and red bell pepper to the wok and stir-fry for 5 minutes.

5 Add the noodles and shrimp to the wok and stir-fry for 2 minutes.

6 In a small bowl, beat together the eggs and coconut milk. Drizzle over the mixture in the wok and stir-fry until the egg sets.

7 Sprinkle the dry unsweetened coconut and chopped fresh cilantro into the wok and toss to mix. Transfer the noodles to warmed serving dishes and serve immediately.

pad thai noodles

serves four

9 oz/250 g rice stick noodles

3 tbsp peanut oil

3 garlic cloves, chopped finely

4 oz/115 g pork tenderloin, chopped
   into ¼-inch/5-mm pieces

1¾ cups cooked shelled shrimp

1 tbsp sugar

3 tbsp Thai fish sauce

1 tbsp tomato catsup

1 tbsp lime juice

2 eggs, beaten

2 cups bean sprouts

TO GARNISH

1 tsp dried red chili flakes

2 scallions, sliced thickly

1 Soak the rice noodles in hot water for about 10 minutes, or according to the package instructions. Drain thoroughly and set aside.

COOK'S TIP

Drain the rice noodles
before adding them to the
pan, as excess moisture
will spoil the texture
of the dish.

2 Heat the peanut oil in a wok or large skillet, add the garlic, and stir-fry over high heat for 30 seconds. Add the pork and stir-fry for about 2–3 minutes, until browned all over.

3 Stir in the shrimp, then add the sugar, fish sauce, catsup, and lime juice, and continue stir-frying for an additional 30 seconds.

4 Stir in the eggs and stir-fry until lightly set. Stir in the noodles, then add the bean sprouts, and stir-fry for 30 seconds to cook lightly.

5 Turn out onto a warmed serving dish and sprinkle with the chili flakes and scallions. Serve immediately.

fried rice with shrimp

serves four

1½ cups long-grain rice

2 eggs

4 tsp cold water

3 tbsp corn oil

4 scallions, sliced thinly on
the diagonal

1 garlic clove, minced

4½ oz/125 g closed-cup or white
mushrooms, sliced thinly

2 tbsp oyster or anchovy sauce

7 oz/200 g canned water chestnuts,
drained and sliced

9 oz/250 g cooked shelled shrimp,
thawed if frozen

salt and pepper

finely chopped parsley, to
garnish (optional)

1 Bring a pan of lightly salted water to a boil. Sprinkle in the rice, return to a boil, then reduce the heat and let simmer for 15–20 minutes, or until tender. Drain, rinse with boiled water, then drain again. Keep warm.

2 Beat each egg separately with 2 teaspoons of cold water and salt and pepper.

3 Heat 2 teaspoons of corn oil in a wok or a large skillet, swirling it around until it is really hot. Pour in the first egg, swirl it around, and cook undisturbed until set. Remove to a plate or a board and repeat with the second egg. Cut the omelets into 1-inch/2.5-cm squares and set aside until required.

4 Heat the remaining oil in the wok, and when it is really hot, add the scallions and garlic and stir-fry for 1 minute. Add the mushrooms and stir-fry for an additional 2 minutes.

5 Stir in the oyster or anchovy sauce, and season with salt and pepper. Add the water chestnuts and shrimp, and stir-fry for 2 minutes.

6 Stir in the cooked rice and stir-fry for 1 minute, then add the omelet squares and stir-fry for 1–2 minutes more, or until piping hot. Serve immediately, garnished with chopped parsley, if you like.

crispy rice noodles

serves four

vegetable oil for deep-frying, plus
   1½ tbsp for stir-frying

7 oz/200 g rice vermicelli noodles

1 onion, chopped finely

4 garlic cloves, chopped finely

1 skinless, boneless chicken breast
   portion, chopped finely

2 fresh red bird-eye chiles, seeded
   and sliced

3 tbsp dried shrimp

4 tbsp dried Chinese black mushrooms,
   soaked, drained, and thinly sliced

4 scallions, sliced

3 tbsp lime juice

2 tbsp light soy sauce

2 tbsp Thai fish sauce

2 tbsp rice vinegar

2 tbsp soft light brown sugar

2 eggs, beaten

3 tbsp chopped fresh cilantro

scallion curls, to garnish

1 Heat the oil in a large wok or skillet until very hot and deep-fry the noodles quickly, occasionally turning them, until puffed up, crisp, and pale golden brown. Lift onto paper towels and drain well. Discard the oil.

2 Heat 1 tablespoon of the oil and stir-fry the onion and garlic for 1 minute. Add the chicken and stir-fry for 3 minutes. Add the chiles, dried shrimp, mushrooms, and scallions.

3 Mix the lime juice, soy sauce, fish sauce, rice vinegar, and sugar, then stir into the wok or skillet and cook for 1 minute. Remove from the heat.

4 Heat the remaining oil in a wide pan and pour in the eggs to coat the bottom of the pan evenly, making a thin omelet. Cook until set and golden, then turn it over, and cook the other side. Turn out and roll up, then slice into long ribbon strips.

5 Toss together the fried noodles, stir-fried ingredients, cilantro, and omelet strips. Garnish with scallion curls and serve immediately.

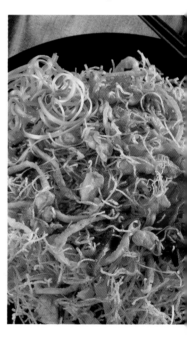

twice-cooked lamb with noodles

serves four

9 oz/250 g egg noodles

1 lb/450 g lamb loin fillet,
    sliced thinly

2 tbsp dark soy sauce

2 tbsp corn oil

2 garlic cloves, minced

1 tbsp superfine sugar

2 tbsp oyster sauce

6 oz/175 g baby spinach

COOK'S TIP

If using dried noodles, follow
the instructions on the package
as they require less soaking.

1 Place the egg noodles in a large bowl and pour over enough boiling water to cover. Set aside to soak for about 10 minutes, or according to the package instructions.

2 Bring a large pan of water to a boil. Add the lamb and cook for 5 minutes. Drain thoroughly.

3 Place the slices of lamb in a bowl and mix with the soy sauce and 1 tablespoon of the corn oil.

4 Heat the remaining corn oil in a large preheated wok, swirling the oil around until it is really hot.

5 Add the marinated lamb and minced garlic to the wok and stir-fry for about 5 minutes, or until the meat is just starting to brown.

6 Add the superfine sugar and oyster sauce to the wok and stir well to mix.

7 Drain the noodles thoroughly. Add the noodles to the wok and stir-fry for an additional 5 minutes.

8 Add the spinach to the wok and cook for 1 minute, or until the leaves just wilt. Transfer the lamb and noodles to serving bowls and serve hot.

chinese vegetable rice

serves four

1¾ cups long-grain white rice

1 tsp ground turmeric

2 tbsp corn oil

8 oz/225 g zucchini, sliced

1 red bell pepper, seeded and sliced

1 green bell pepper, seeded and sliced

1 fresh green chile, seeded and
   finely chopped

1 medium carrot, grated coarsely

1½ cups bean sprouts

6 scallions, sliced, plus extra to
   garnish (optional)

2 tbsp light soy sauce

salt

COOK'S TIP

For real luxury, add a few saffron
threads steeped in boiling water
instead of the turmeric.

---

1 Place the rice and turmeric in a pan of lightly salted water and bring to a boil. Reduce the heat and let simmer for 12–15 minutes, until the rice is just tender. Drain the rice thoroughly and press out any excess water with paper towels. Set aside until required.

2 Heat the corn oil in a large preheated wok.

3 Add the zucchini to the wok and stir-fry for about 2 minutes.

4 Add the bell peppers and chile and stir-fry for 2–3 minutes.

5 Add the cooked rice to the wok, a little at a time, tossing well after each addition.

6 Add the carrots, bean sprouts, and scallions to the wok and stir-fry for an additonal 2 minutes.

7 Drizzle with soy sauce and serve immediately, garnished with extra scallions, if you like.

thai-style noodle rostis

serves four

4½ oz/125 g vermicelli rice noodles

2 scallions, shredded finely

1 lemongrass stalk, shredded finely

3 tbsp finely shredded fresh coconut

vegetable oil for cooking

fresh red chiles, to garnish

TO SERVE

generous 1 cup bean sprouts

1 small red onion, sliced thinly

1 avocado, peeled, pitted, and
   thinly sliced

2 tbsp lime juice

2 tbsp Chinese rice wine

1 tsp chili sauce

1 Break the rice noodles into short pieces and soak in hot water for 4 minutes, or according to the package instructions. Drain thoroughly and pat dry with paper towels.

2 Mix the drained noodles, scallions, lemongrass, and shredded coconut.

3 Heat a small amount of oil until very hot in a wok or heavy skillet. Brush a 3½-inch/9-cm round cookie cutter with oil and place in the wok. Spoon a small amount of noodle mixture into the cutter to just cover the bottom of the wok, then press down lightly with the back of a spoon.

4 Cook for 30 seconds, then carefully remove the cutter, and continue cooking the rosti until it is golden brown, turning it over once. Remove and drain on paper towels. Repeat with the remaining noodles, to make about 12 rostis.

5 To serve, arrange the noodles in stacks, with bean sprouts, onion, and avocado between the layers.

6 Mix the lime juice, rice wine, and chili sauce and spoon over the stacks just before serving, garnished with the red chiles.

rice noodles with spinach

serves four

4 oz/115 g thin rice stick noodles

2 tbsp dried shrimp, optional

9 oz/250 g baby spinach leaves

1 tbsp peanut oil

2 garlic cloves, chopped finely

2 tsp Thai green curry paste

1 tsp sugar

1 tbsp light soy sauce

COOK'S TIP

It is best to choose young spinach leaves for this dish, as they are beautifully tender and cook within a matter of seconds. If you can only get older spinach, however, shred the leaves before adding to the dish so they cook more quickly.

1 Soak the noodles in hot water for 15 minutes, or according to the package instructions, then drain well.

2 Put the dried shrimp (if using) in a bowl and add hot water to cover. Set aside to soak for 10 minutes, then drain.

3 Wash the baby spinach thoroughly, drain well, and pat dry. Remove any tough stalks.

4 Heat the oil in a preheated wok or large, heavy skillet and stir-fry the garlic for 1 minute. Stir in the curry paste and stir-fry for 30 seconds. Stir in the soaked shrimp (if using) and stir-fry for 30 seconds.

5 Add the spinach and stir-fry for 1–2 minutes, until the leaves are just wilted.

6 Stir in the sugar and soy sauce, then add the noodles, and toss thoroughly to mix. transfer to a warmed platter and serve immediately.

drunken noodles

serves four

6 oz/175 g rice stick noodles

2 tbsp vegetable oil

1 garlic clove, minced

2 small fresh green chiles, chopped

1 small onion, sliced thinly

5½ oz/150 g lean ground pork

1 small green bell pepper, seeded
   and finely chopped

4 kaffir lime leaves, shredded finely

1 tbsp dark soy sauce

1 tbsp light soy sauce

½ tsp sugar

1 tomato, cut into thin wedges

2 tbsp fresh sweet basil leaves,
   finely shredded, to garnish

TO SERVE

salad greens

radishes

1 Soak the noodles in hot water for 15 minutes, or according to the package instructions. Drain well.

2 Heat the vegetable oil in a preheated wok and stir-fry the garlic, chiles, and onion for 1 minute.

3 Stir in the ground pork and stir-fry over high heat for 1 minute, then add the green bell pepper, and continue stir-frying for an additional 2 minutes.

4 Stir in the lime leaves, soy sauces, and sugar. Add the noodles and tomato and toss well to heat thoroughly.

5 Sprinkle with basil and serve with salad greens and radishes.

COOK'S TIP

Fresh kaffir lime leaves freeze well, so if you buy more than you need, simply tie them in a tightly sealed plastic freezer bag and freeze for up to a month. They can be used straight from the freezer.

chile shrimp noodles

serves four

2 tbsp light soy sauce

1 tbsp lime or lemon juice

1 tbsp Thai fish sauce

125 g/4½ oz firm bean curd
   (drained weight)

125 g/4½ oz cellophane noodles

2 tbsp corn oil

4 shallots, sliced thinly

2 garlic cloves, minced

1 small fresh red chile, seeded and
   finely chopped

2 celery stalks, sliced thinly

2 carrots, sliced thinly

⅔ cup cooked shelled shrimp

1 cup bean sprouts

TO GARNISH

celery leaves

fresh chiles

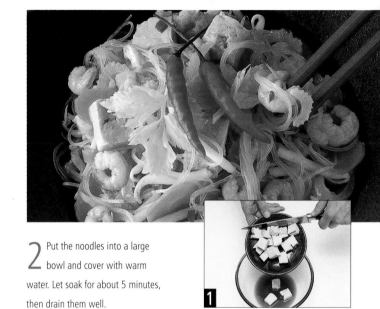

1 Mix the light soy sauce, lime or lemon juice, and fish sauce in a small bowl. Using a sharp knife, cut the bean curd into ½–¾-inch/1–2-cm cubes. Add them to the bowl and toss until coated all over in the soy sauce mixture. Cover the bowl with plastic wrap and set aside for about 15 minutes to marinate.

2 Put the noodles into a large bowl and cover with warm water. Let soak for about 5 minutes, then drain them well.

3 Heat the corn oil in a preheated wok or large heavy skillet. Add the shallots, garlic, and red chile, and stir-fry for 1 minute.

4 Add the sliced celery and carrots to the wok or skillet and stir-fry for an additional 2–3 minutes.

5 Tip the drained noodles into the wok or skillet and cook, stirring constantly, for 2 minutes, then add the shrimp, bean sprouts, and marinated bean curd, with the soy sauce mixture.

Cook over medium–high heat, stirring frequently, for 2–3 minutes, until heated through.

6 Transfer the mixture in the wok to a warmed serving dish, garnish with celery leaves and fresh chiles, and serve immediately.

cellophane noodles & shrimp

serves four

175 g/6 oz cellophane noodles

1 tbsp vegetable oil

1 garlic clove, minced

2 tsp grated fresh gingerroot

24 raw jumbo shrimp, shelled

1 red bell pepper, seeded and
    thinly sliced

1 green bell pepper, seeded and
    thinly sliced

1 onion, chopped

2 tbsp light soy sauce

juice of 1 orange

2 tsp wine vinegar

pinch of brown sugar

⅔ cup fish bouillon

1 tbsp cornstarch

2 tsp water

orange slices, to garnish

1 Cook the noodles in a pan of boiling water for 1 minute. Drain well, rinse, and drain again.

2 Heat the vegetable oil in a preheated wok. Stir-fry the garlic and ginger for 30 seconds.

3 Add the shrimp and stir-fry for 2 minutes. Remove with a slotted spoon and keep warm.

4 Add the bell peppers and onion to the wok and stir-fry for 2 minutes. Stir in the soy sauce, orange juice, vinegar, sugar, and bouillon. Return the shrimp to the wok and cook for 8–10 minutes, until cooked through.

5 Blend the cornstarch with the water and stir into the wok. Bring to a boil, add the noodles, and cook for 1–2 minutes. Garnish and serve.

stir-fried japanese mushroom noodles

serves four

8 oz/225 g Japanese egg noodles

2 tbsp corn oil

1 red onion, sliced

1 garlic clove, minced

1 lb/450 g mixed mushrooms
   (shiitake, oyster, brown cap),
   wiped and sliced

12 oz/350 g bok choy

2 tbsp sweet sherry

6 tbsp oyster sauce

4 scallions, sliced

1 tbsp toasted sesame seeds

COOK'S TIP

The variety of mushrooms in
large food stores has improved
and a good mixture should
be easily obtainable. If not,
use the more common white
and flat mushrooms.

1 Place the Japanese egg noodles in a large bowl. Pour over enough boiling water to cover and let the noodles soak for 10 minutes.

2 Heat the corn oil in a large preheated wok.

3 Add the red onion and garlic to the wok and stir-fry for 2–3 minutes, or until softened.

4 Add the mushrooms to the wok and stir-fry for about 5 minutes, or until the mushrooms have softened.

5 Tip the egg noodles into a strainer and drain thoroughly.

6 Add the the bok choy, drained noodles, sweet sherry, and oyster sauce to the wok. Toss all of the ingredients together until mixed and stir-fry for 2–3 minutes, or until the liquid is just bubbling.

7 Transfer the mushroom noodles to warmed serving bowls and sprinkle with sliced scallions and toasted sesame seeds. Serve.

rice noodles with mushrooms & bean curd

serves four

8 oz/225 g rice stick noodles

2 tbsp peanut oil

1 garlic clove, chopped finely

¾-inch/2-cm piece fresh gingerroot,
    finely chopped

4 shallots, sliced thinly

1 cup sliced shiitake mushrooms

3½ oz/100 g firm bean curd
    (drained weight), cut into
    small dice

2 tbsp light soy sauce

1 tbsp Chinese rice wine

1 tbsp Thai fish sauce

1 tbsp smooth peanut butter

1 tsp chili sauce

2 tbsp toasted peanuts, chopped

shredded fresh basil leaves, to serve

1 Soak the noodles in hot water for 15 minutes, or according to the package instructions. Drain well.

COOK'S TIP

For an easy pantry dish, replace the fresh shiitake mushrooms with a can of well-drained Chinese straw mushrooms.

2 Heat the oil in a preheated wok. Add the garlic, ginger, and shallots and stir-fry for 1–2 minutes, until softened and lightly browned.

3 Add the shiitake mushrooms and stir-fry over medium heat for an additional 2–3 minutes. Stir in the bean curd and toss to brown lightly.

4 Mix the soy sauce, rice wine, fish sauce, peanut butter, and chili sauce, then stir into the wok.

5 Stir in the rice noodles and toss to coat evenly in the sauce. Sprinkle with peanuts and shredded basil leaves and serve hot.

chicken chow mein

serves four

9 oz/250 g medium egg noodles

2 tbsp corn oil

9½ oz/275 g cooked chicken breast
  portions, shredded

1 garlic clove, chopped finely

1 red bell pepper, seeded and
  thinly sliced

3½ oz/100 g shiitake
  mushrooms, sliced

6 scallions, sliced

1 cup bean sprouts

3 tbsp light soy sauce

1 tbsp sesame oil

1 Slightly break up the egg noodles, then place in a large bowl or dish. Pour over sufficient boiling water to cover and set aside to soak for about 10 minutes.

2 Heat the corn oil in a large preheated wok. Add the shredded chicken, finely chopped garlic, bell pepper slices, mushrooms, scallions, and bean sprouts to the wok and stir-fry for about 5 minutes.

3 Tip the noodles into a strainer and drain thoroughly. Add the noodles to the wok, toss well, and stir-fry for an additional 5 minutes.

4 Drizzle the soy sauce and sesame oil over the chow mein and toss until well mixed.

5 Transfer the chicken chow mein to warmed individual serving bowls and serve immediately.

VARIATION

You can make the chow mein with a selection of vegetables for a vegetarian dish, if you like.

stir-fried cod & mango with noodles

serves four

9 oz/250 g egg noodles

1 lb/450 g cod fillet, skinned

1 tbsp paprika

2 tbsp corn oil

1 red onion, sliced

1 orange bell pepper, seeded
   and sliced

1 green bell pepper, seeded
   and sliced

3½ oz/100 g baby corn cobs, halved

1 mango, peeled, pitted, and sliced

1 cup bean sprouts

2 tbsp tomato catsup

2 tbsp light soy sauce

2 tbsp medium sherry

1 tsp cornstarch

1 Place the egg noodles in a large bowl and cover with boiling water. Let stand for about 10 minutes.

2 Rinse the cod fillet and pat dry with paper towels. Cut the cod flesh into thin strips.

3 Place the cod strips in a large bowl. Add the paprika and toss well to coat the fish.

4 Heat the corn oil in a large preheated wok.

5 Add the onion, bell peppers, and baby corn cobs to the wok and stir-fry for about 5 minutes.

6 Add the cod to the wok together with the sliced mango and stir-fry for an additional 2–3 minutes, or until the fish is tender.

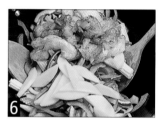

7 Add the bean sprouts to the wok and toss well to mix.

8 Mix the tomato catsup, soy sauce, sherry, and cornstarch in a small bowl. Add the mixture to the wok and cook, stirring occasionally, until the juices thicken.

9 Drain the noodles thoroughly and transfer to warmed serving bowls. Transfer the cod and mango stir-fry to separate warmed serving bowls and serve immediately.